Faith Of Our Mothers

Faith Of
Our Mothers

*A Series of Monologues of The Mothers In
The Genealogy of Jesus
And
Other Women of Strong Faith*

LaNell Johnson

CSS Publishing Company, Inc.
Lima, Ohio

Library of Congress Cataloging-in-Publication Data

Names: Johnson, LaNell, 1943- author.
Title: Faith of our mothers : a series of monologues of the mothers in the
    genealogy of Jesus and other women of strong faith / LaNell Johnson.
Description: First edition. | Lima, Ohio : CSS Publishing Company, Inc.,
    2022.
Identifiers: LCCN 2022001482 (print) | LCCN 2022001483 (ebook) | ISBN
    9780788030345 | ISBN 9780788030352 (ebook)
Subjects: LCSH: Mothers--Biblical teaching. | Mothers--Religious life. |
    Women in Christianity.
Classification: LCC BS579.M65 J64 2022 (print) | LCC BS579.M65 (ebook) |
    DDC 220.83068743--dc23/eng/20220216
LC record available at https://lccn.loc.gov/2022001482
LC ebook record available at https://lccn.loc.gov/2022001483

For more information about CSS Publishing Company resources, visit our website at www. csspub.com, email us at csr@csspub.com, or call (800) 241-4056.

e-book:
ISBN-13: 978-0-7880-3035-2
ISBN-10: 0-7880-3035-3

ISBN-13: 978-0-7880-3034-5
ISBN-10: 0-7880-3034-5   DIGITALLY PRINTED

CONTENTS Of MONOLOGUES

Mothers In The Genealogy Of Jesus

OTHER WOMEN OF FAITH

PROLOGUE

"All mankind is of one author, and is one volume; when one man dies, one chapter is not torn out of the book, but translated into a better language: and every chapter must be so translated.... But God's hand is in every translation; and his hand shall bind up all our scattered leaves again, for that library where every book shall lie open to one another.

"For no man is an island; entire of itself; every man is a piece of the continent, a part of the main... Any man's death diminishes me, because I am involved in mankind; and therefore, never send to know for whom the bell tolls; it tolls for thee."[1]

These words written by John Donne in 1630, expressed beautifully that we are all part of the "clan of Man." And we share a kinship with those who lived before, those who lived in the distant past, those who lived in Bible times, and those who lived in the not-so-distant past.

This kinship is kept alive through the story. Elie Wiesel, recipient of the 1986 Nobel Peace Prize, recounted the importance of story as he recounts a rabbinical tale of rabbis in subsequent generations, who over time forget the sacred place, how to light the sacred fire and pray the sacred prayer, until finally the last rabbi admits sitting in his armchair, his head in his hands, calling out to God; "I cannot find the place in the forest, or light the fire or say the prayer. All I can do is tell the story and this must be sufficient." And it was sufficient. Then Wiesel asked the question, "Are we in danger of losing our story?"[2]

Henri Nouwen reminded us that we need to become storytellers again. He wrote: "One of the remarkable qualities of the story is that it creates space. We can dwell in the story, walk around, find our own place. The story confronts but does not oppress; the story inspires, but does not manipulate. The story invites us to an encounter, a dialogue, a mutual sharing.

1 John Donne, "Devotions Upon Emergent Occasions", Meditation XVII in Complete Poetry and Selected Prose of John Donne and Complete Works of William Blake (New York: Random House, 1941), 331.
2 [Elie Wiesel, *The Goates of the Forest*, transl. by Frances Frenaye (New York: Holt, Rinehart & Winston, Inc., 1968)].

"A story that guides is a story that opens the door and offers a space in which to search and boundaries to help us find what we seek, but it does not tell us what to do or how to do it. The story brings us into touch with the vision and so guides us... As long as we have stories to tell each other there is hope. As long as we can remind each other of the lives of men and women in whom the love of God becomes manifest, there is reason to move forward to a new land in which new stories are hidden."[3]

These monologues offer such a story; a place to visit, to browse, to confront old familiar characters and enter into dialogue with them, to expand the story beyond the written page. You are invited into a scene, an event, and emotion, and therefore able to experience the truth for yourself.

The greatest limitation to the power of the biblical story is that, down through the centuries, we have glorified, deified, the characters until they are so far removed from human emotion that it is difficult to identify with them. In this series of monologues, I have retold the old stories in a way in which the characters are real, live, flesh and blood people not so different from us. They experience joy and sorrow, good and evil fortune. They experience family and financial problems. They are plagued with questions of the meaning of life.

Sometimes their acceptance of the culture around them, such as human sacrifice, seem very strange to us. Yet their explanations, their stories of faith, have survived the centuries. In this work I have interwoven the biblical account, some archaeological discoveries, new scientific data, as well as pure fiction. Perhaps truth lies in the combination of all these factors. I have also tried to lift up the importance of the genealogies, which we tend to skip over, as we search for the continuity of God's involvement in human affairs.

I have written the monologues in conversational English rather than the more proper grammatical structure, so that the listener may "hear" the words more easily. The monologues can be performed without memorization or costume. However, they can become so much more. These monologues can become an effective way of sharing God's word in a new and fresh way. In

3 Henri J. M. Nouwen, *The Living Reminder*, (Minneapolis, Minn.: Seabury Press, Inc., 1977).

the words of Isaiah: *The Lord God has given me the tongue of a teacher, that I may know how to sustain the weary with a word.*[4]

Biblical storytelling is not necessarily fact-telling. While it is important to not include anything *contrary* to the biblical account, literary license is acceptable. The original biblical storytellers did this. The most famous example is found in the story of creation. God created Adam (one person). Then, he created Eve (the second person). After that came Cain (the third person) and Abel (the fourth person). Four people in all. But, then, Cain killed Abel. We are now back down to three people. And the scripture states that Cain ran away and took a wife. From where? The storyteller was concerned with sharing the greater truth, not in giving a literal account. As a present-day biblical storyteller, the greater truth is also what we want to share.

These monologues are entertaining, but that is not the main purpose. These monologues are instructive, but that is not the main purpose. These monologues are inspirational, and that is the main purpose.

These monologues offer the listener an opportunity to identify with the character and see how God worked in their lives, and to remind them that God desires to work in yours — is in fact, already working within you. As I said, I have written these monologues in conversational English rather that proper "written" English, so that your 'talk' will sound more natural. I have used quotation marks, italics, capitalization, and parentheses to make it easier for you to convey important distinction of certain words or meanings. I have also used a phrase, here and there, of familiar hymns, so that your audience can become more a part of your story. I have, also, not footnoted much of the scripture, since certain portions of the monologue are heavy scripture. But, I have included in each of the "cover sheets" what scripture you should study before performing.

Remember, again, to pray before performing and claim the promise from Isaiah 55:11, "So shall my word be that goeth forth out of my mouth; it shall not return unto me void, but it shall accomplish that which I please, and it shall prosper in the thing

4 Isaiah 50: 4 (NRSV)

whereto I sent it."

As Paul wrote to Timothy, *I am reminded of your sincere faith, a faith that lived first in your grandmother Lois and your mother Eunice and now, I am sure, lives in you. For this reason, I remind you to rekindle the gift of God that is within you.*[5]

My personal understanding of God, my own brand of theology has shown through. I do not apologize for this. My theology differs from yours, and well it should. No one individual, no one denomination, no one faith can contain all the truth of God. Understanding comes as we open up, expose, and share our views with one another. As we immerse ourselves in the great stories of our faith, the *Faith Of Our Mothers*, the ears of our understanding are opened and we can hear the voice of God.

I invite you, now, to come and share the "story",and may God's Word go with you as you speak

5 2 Timothy 1:5-6 (NRSV).

USAGES FOR THESE MONOLOGUES:

1) Women's church group

2) Wednesday night fellowship dinner and program

3) Senior citizens fellowships

4) Weekend spiritual retreat: "Tell Me the Story of Jesus"
   First session: 'Mother Mary' (the Christmas Story)
   Second session: 'Mother Mary' (the crucifixion story)
   (The two Mother Marys would need be presented by the same person)
   Third session: 'Mary Magdalene' (the resurrection story)

5) Six-week series on Sunday Morning or Sunday Night Lenten series.
   Monologues to cover seven characters in the genealogy of Jesus; Eve, Naamah, Sarah, Leah, Rahab, Ruth, Mother Mary
   Monologues can even be used in a revival setting. I was invited to lead a three night revival as a different character each night, complete with costume, and ending each night with an altar call from the character.

6) The last portion of Mary Magdalene can be used for outdoor Easter Sunrise Service

TIPS FOR DELIVERING MONOLOGUES

1. <u>PRAY</u> first.

2. Then <u>LEARN</u> the material. Don't take my word for the scriptural account of the story, read the scripture for yourself. Using several different translations is good. While the Living Bible is not the most accurate version, it is often good to give a fresh view. But, <u>before</u> studying the scripture for your character, pray the prayer of illumination: **Lord, open our hearts and minds by the power of your Holy Spirit, that, as the scriptures are read and your word proclaimed, we may hear with joy what you say to us today. Amen.** Then, become that character. Only then, begin to <u>MEMORIZE</u>. Then, you are ready to <u>TELL</u> her story.

3. Remember, memorizing is better than reading. But, telling is better than memorizing.

4. Just before performing, pray again. Pray silently the prayer from Psalm 19:14; **May the words of my mouth and the meditation of my heart be acceptable in thy sight, O Lord, my strength and my redeemer.**

5. Research the culture. Because I was a Christian educator many years before becoming ordained, I try to give what cultural facts seem appropriate. Much information can be found on the internet. But, be careful. Not everything on the internet is correct. But, the more you research personally, the more you "own" the material.

6. Monologues can be performed without memorizing or in costume. You may simply read from the printed page. If you are reading, enlarge font to twenty or more, if necessary, so you will not need

to use glasses and you can stand behind podium. If you wish to perform in costume, you may begin your collection from the costumes your church uses for the Nativity play.

7. But, try to always, at least, wear a head drape, measuring approximately 72" x 24". And always remove eye glasses and wrist watch, and wear rings only of metal (gold or silver) not with gem setting. Patterns for "pinner" and "mob" hats for Susanna Wesley can be found on line.

8. The monologues vary in length. A 3,000 word count is approximately twenty minutes of performance time. Adjust them to fit your time frame. If the monologue is too long, simply pick the portion you like best and leave out the other portions. If it is too short, read the biblical passage again and elaborate on a point or do additional research and add in the new material you found.

9. If you get to a point and you realize you have left out a crucial part of the story, do what you usually do in a conversation, stop and say, "Oh, I forgot. I left out an important part," then add the omitted portion and go on with the story.

10. Feel free to end the monologue in a way that best fits your situation.

11. If used in a worship setting with hymns, select hymns that your audience knows well. And, for the closing hymn, chose one that is appropriate to the way you end your monologue.

12. Use rectangular wicker basket, approximately 6"x10"x13", with hinged lid for props. Certain quotes which need to be used word-for-word, can be taped on inside lid to be read, if needed.

13. Stay adaptable with the printed material. For example, when performing Rahab at a church I had not attended before, I noticed a large pile of bricks in the far corner of the parking lot. Once inside, I casually asked about the bricks and was told that they were from the old chapel they had torn down while making renovations. They were planning to create some kind of memorial to the memory of those who had gone before. I immediately asked for a Bible and did a quick study on the chapter beyond what I was planning on covering, when Joshua instructed twelve men to construct a monument of twelve stones at the spot where God stopped the River Jordan so they could cross over.

I added to my monologue that Rahab questioned why the people were slowing down as they passed a pile of rocks and were told that it was a monument of remembrance, (I said) similar to your pile of bricks which you are planning to construct as a monument of remembrance. My audience was very pleased that I had included that mention in my monologue.

14. In making your story seem more real and current, you can add "off the cuff" remarks, such as, when the wedding host ran out of wine, you might say, " I don't know what it would be like in your day, but for this poor host, it was a great social faux pas!" Your audience can relate to that feeling.

15. Use the printed monologue as a guideline. If you know the story, or if the written words seem awkward to you — Tell it in your own words. The monologues are not a dialogue script where you mess up the other's response if you change a line. And, I rarely present the material in exactly the same way twice.

16. For some reason, it is said that dark lipstick helps the listeners "hear" you better.

17. If performing several characters in a row, it is best not to heavily rehearse the others until the first one is performed.

18. As an aid to memorization, retype the printed monologue. The discipline of typing it yourself greatly aids in memorization. It also offers the opportunity to increase font size if you need to look at the material from time to time during performance. It also offers the advantage to change some of the wording that seems awkward to you. And, it offers you the opportunity to scale back or enhance the material to fit your time frame.

19. Have fun in the fabric store:

– Before making any costumes, you might want to check the nativity costumes your church uses each year.

– Pick three or four solid, cotton materials for the basic robes (blue, brown, rose, musty green). No pastels, no black, white or cream color.

– Pick material for head wrap that complements the color of the robes. Select two for each robe, one solid, one striped. No flowered, patterned, print or geometrics.

– Select light-weight stretch satin or cotton. No silky fabric because it will slide off hair. Do not select heavy material because the weight will also cause it to slide off head.

– For Eve and Esther costumes, look for brown ribbed knit. Sometimes, you can find this material in 'tube' fashion.

- For sheep skin, look for faux fur that has texture of lamb, not long hair. Pick cream color — not white, black or pattered.

- For belts: rope can be found in "cords' section or can use either gold or silver metal belt.

- Pattern books contain a section on costumes. The biblical costumes are usually at the very back of the book.

- Both Eve and Esther need to be strapless; Eve's to just above knees with belt of 'vine', Esther's to floor length with gold rope or metal belt for belt. A fabric of gold lame can be used around the shoulders.

- Packets of multi-colored rhinestones can be found in 'crafts' section. These can be glued onto 'gold' and 'silver' goblets from the party store. Also, glued onto gold headband worn across forehead instead of in hair.

20. Also, have fun in party supply store:

- Gold and silver goblets. (Goblets for Esther of silver and gold can be hard to find. Pewter can be used for silver; copper may be used for gold. Sometimes found in world bazaar type stores. Occasionally, a high-end party supply store that carries gold and silver 'paper' party trays, etc.)

- Bow from toy bow and arrow kit (remove string and wrap bow in "rainbow" hair scrunchies and restring)

- Gold scepter from king's section

- Mini insects (frogs, grasshoppers, flies). May have to buy whole bag to get just the right insect.

EVE

Character: *Eve*

Caption: *The Mother Of All Mothers*

Publicity Blurb: *"Can you imagine what I felt like when my husband, the only man in the world for me, blamed me for everything that went wrong?"*

Scripture Reading: *Genesis 3:13,16a, 20; 4:1-2a, 8, 25-26*

Hymns: *"Morning Has Broken"; "This Is My Father's World"; "Trust and Obey"; "Precious Lord, Take My Hand"; "Spirit of God, Descend Upon My Heart"*

Scripture Study Prep: *Genesis, Chapters 1 – 4*

Length of Performance: *word count 2,429*

Dress: *short, brown, strapless, tube knit garment*

Hair: *hair washed and "scrounged" only*

Shoes: *barefoot*

Accessories: *flowers in hair (some stretchy headbands come with flowers attached); wooden necklace and bracelet; belt of vine of flowers*

Props: *apple and other artificial fruit in flowerpot liner; faux sheep skin — reprints from* Newsweek, *January 11, 1988, pages 46-52 and* Discover, *August. 1990, pages 52-59, both of which carry cover stories of scientists searching for the original Eve from whom we all descended.*

Make-up: *usual*

Suggested Season to Perform: *Earth Day; Mother's Day*

Eve

The Mother Of All Mothers

My name is Eve. My husband calls me that because it means 'Mother of All Living'. So I guess that makes us all related. I don't quite know where to begin telling my story, because I seem to have started my life somewhere in midstream. My first memory is of seeing my husband. I didn't know he was my husband. I didn't know he was a man. I had never seen anything or anyone before. But the moment I saw him, I loved him.

He explained to me about God and how God created the beautiful garden we were in. Adam said God created all the plants and animals, as well as the two of us. I didn't understand much of what he said. But Adam made sure I understood God's *one* commandment — to not eat the fruit of a very special tree. The special tree was called the tree of the knowledge of good and evil. God told Adam that we would die if we ate of its fruit. It really didn't matter, because we had more than enough to eat. But, secretly, I wondered if I might like that fruit. But I obeyed my husband and my God.

Life was wonderful in the garden. We were never sick, never wanted for anything. My husband and I loved each other very much. Everything was perfect. In the cool of the evening, God would come down and walk and talk with Adam the way good friends should and do. Then Adam would tell me all that he had learned from God that day. I guess everything would have stayed perfect forever — if it hadn't been for me.

Although I obeyed God's command and never even touched the forbidden tree, it was as though the tree casted a spell over me. I found more and more excuses to walk by. This special tree looked different from all the rest. There were other trees in the garden that were more majestic. But this tree was perfectly shaped, its boughs bent low to the ground with luscious fruit of many different colors and shapes. As I would stare at the tree, I would try to imagine what the different colors and shapes tasted like. *(hold up different fruits)*

One day, after I had looked at the tree for a while, I turned to walk away when I heard my name called. This was very strange because the voice was not Adam's or God's. And there was no one else in all creation. The voice was coming from that tree. Of course, I had to investigate. The voice seemed to be coming from that special tree. Cautiously, I approach the tree. I stared into its depths and saw some leaves rustling. I stepped closer. And then, I saw it — a creature unlike any other creature I had ever seen. Its skin was silky and shiny, brilliantly colored, almost iridescent. Though beautiful and alluring, a sense of danger emanated from its long and sinuous body.

"Who are you?" I said to myself.

"A friend," it answered. That really freaked me out. In all creation, no animal ever spoke. I wanted to run, but I stood transfixed. I was interested, excited, but frightened.

"Here, take a bite," the creature said, as he offered me an apple. *(hold up apple)*

"Oh, no! God said we would die if we ate of this tree," I explained.

"But that's not true." the creature answered. "God lied. Look, I'm eating this fruit and it isn't hurting me."

"But, why would God lie?" I asked.

"Do you know the name of this tree?"

"Yes," I replied. "It is the tree of the knowledge of good and evil."

"Exactly! The tree of the *knowledge*. Because this fruit is not only delicious, but it opens your eyes, opens your mind. It makes you smart — so smart you will be as smart as God. And, God doesn't want that. Go on, try it. I promise you'll like it. Just one bite. What harm could it do?"

He seemed to make sense, so I hesitantly reached out and plucked a fruit from the tree. My hands trembled as I raised the forbidden fruit to my mouth. "Just one bite," I thought, "what harm could it do?" (take bite)

The fruit had a kind of bitter-sweetness about it. Not exactly delicious, but, more importantly, what the creature had said was true. Suddenly, I could feel my mind expanding. I understood more than I ever had before. I instantly wanted more and more. When I had eaten my fill, I picked up an arm-full for Adam. (*Fill up basket of assorted fruits*) That night when he returned to our bower, I told him what I had done. Adam was horrified!

"Oh Eve!" he cried. "What have you done? Now you will die!"

"No, Adam," I replied, "that's where you're wrong. God lied to us. The creature over by the tree had eaten of the fruit for a long time, and I ate my fill this afternoon. It didn't hurt either of us. And, even better, it makes your mind almost explode with knowledge. Please, try it. Just one bite, for me, Adam, if you love me. Please."

(go pick up apple and extend it to Adam)

Reluctantly, Adam took a bite and he found the taste as appealing as I had. His eyes and his mind were opened. We made our evening meal on the forbidden, intoxicating fruit. Then, suddenly, we heard God approaching. You see, in the excitement of gorging ourselves on that forbidden fruit, we had forgotten about God.

"Hurry," whispered Adam. "God must not find us here with the fruit or see us naked." Adam grabbed my hand and quickly, but quietly, we sneaked into the bushes to hide.

"Adam, where are you?" God called as his presence filled the garden.

With quivering voice Adam answered, "We're here, Lord, in the bushes."

"What are you doing in the bushes, Adam?"

"We're hiding from you, Lord." Adam replied.

"Why are you hiding from me, Adam? Aren't we friends?"

"Oh, yes, Lord, we are friends," my husband said, "but we're naked and we didn't want you to see our nakedness."

God's voice became stern, thundering so loud that the ground shook as he spoke. "Who told you that you were naked, Adam? Come and stand before me and answer my question."

I don't think I've ever been more scared in all my life. I took Adam's hand and, timidly, we step forward, our heads bowed.

"Who told you that you were naked?" repeated God.

"Well, you see, God..." my Adam stammered.

"You have eaten of the forbidden fruit. You have eaten of the tree of the knowledge of good and evil. Adam! Adam! What have you done? I warned you not to disobey me."

"Yes, God, and I truly meant to obey you. But, you see, this woman," he said pointing over to me, "this woman you made for me — she made me do it."

I could not believe my ears. I could not believe that my husband, my lover, the only man on earth for me, (literally), was willing to put all the blame on me. I tell you I was plenty scared. God had said that the punishment for eating the fruit was death. I wondered how God would kill me. Would it hurt an awful lot, or would I just fade back into the nothingness from where I had come?

"Eve, Eve, is this true?" God was asking me.

I tried to speak, but I couldn't make a sound.

"I'm waiting, Eve. Did you cause Adam to sin?"

Finally, I found my voice. "But God, it wasn't my fault." I insisted. "There was this creature over by the tree, and he talked me into it. He made me do it." I figured that if Adam could blame me and get away with it, maybe I could blame the strange creature and not get punished.

God's voice was stern and full of wrath as he turned to the alluring creature. "Cursed are you, serpent, from this day forth. And on your belly in the dust shall you crawl!"

I watched as this beautiful creature plopped to the ground and slithered off. He didn't look very beautiful then. He looked repulsive.

"Whew! — That was a close call," I thought.

But then my heart broke as I heard the sadness in God's voice. "My children, if you only knew what you have done. Now you must leave this garden home. You must go out into a world which will be hostile to you. The grains and berries will grow only by the toil of your hands. And children will be born to you, Eve, only in great pain. Many of the animals which have been your friends will now seek to bring you harm. In all the places you go, there will be discord. Your body will be wracked with pain and disease. You will grow old and finally you will die. Your days will be full of sadness and when you call upon me, though I will always answer, it will be difficult for you to even hear my voice. You must leave, because if you should eat of the forbidden tree of life you would live forever. Now that you have sinned that cannot be allowed. You must leave and I will hide this garden from all humankind."

We stood naked, vulnerable, and ashamed before our God. Then his compassion greatly surprised me. In his love, God went out and killed two of the most beautiful animals of his creation, lambs without spot or blemish. As he slit their throats and the blood soaked into the ground, I heard God speak these words: "And so it shall be, without the shedding of blood there can be no forgiveness of sins."[6] I didn't understand what that meant, but I knew it was important.

After God had killed the animals, he skinned them and fashioned clothing of hides to cover our nakedness. (go pick up lamb skin)

We stood there, covered in the bloody skins for what seemed like forever. We were hoping against hope that God would change his mind, that everything could go back to the way it had been before our terrible act. God had said that there could be no forgiveness without the shedding of blood. Well, blood had been shed.

"Please," I begged. "Please don't make us go. I promise we will never disobey you again. Please!"

I believe right then that God wanted to take us back, to tell us that everything was all right again, that what we had done really didn't matter. But that didn't happen. Softly, and with pain in his voice, God said, "Now, Adam, you and your woman must leave this place. But never forget that my love goes with you."

With those words we turned and, hand-in-hand, walked toward the gate (a gate I had never seen before) leading out of the Garden of Eden and into the outside world.

As we approached the gate, to my horror I saw two large apparitions seated above the gate. These beings were frightening, but also really beautiful. Light radiated from their bodies.

6 Hebrews 9:22 (NRSV)

"What are they?" I asked in a hushed whisper.

"Beings from another part of God's creation. I think they live where God dwells."

"Do we have to go under them?" I asked, absolutely petrified. "Couldn't we find a way around?"

"They won't hurt us," Adam said. "They're only here to make sure we leave and never attempt to return."

Fearfully, we stepped through the gate. After we had taken a few steps, I looked back. And to my horror I saw a gigantic, flaming sword suspended in the air, constantly rotating, — permanently sealing access to the tree of life. At the sight of the sword, we ran and took cover. I don't know how long we crouched hidden among the rocks. Finally, with our limbs aching from our awkward hiding positions, we ventured out into the open.

All seem peaceful and quiet. We looked back toward the garden, but could see nothing — not the flaming sword, not the angels, not the gate, not even the garden. We were all alone on the earth. We wandered the earth for a long, long time. And God's words came true. The animals and the weather conspired against us. It was only through hard work that Adam was able to eke out a living from the soil. God's words to me came true. In time, I gave birth to two children, both boys. And God's promise was indeed true. There was pain. Great pain!

But, years later, I experienced pain even greater than that of childbirth. My oldest son murdered my youngest son and then ran away. In one short day, I lost both my children. My grief was almost more than I could bear. For days I wept uncontrollably. "Oh, Adam, I am to blame for everything. All that has happened is my fault. My sin — my sin!" I cried, accepting the full blame for my sin in the garden.

Putting his arm comfortingly around me, my husband said. "Yes, your sin was great, but, my sin was my own, and Cain's sin was his own. God has forgiven us, though we must live with the consequences of those sins. You and I still have one another, and we still have our God. Somehow we will survive and will create a good life for ourselves out here in this hostile land."

And we did. Years later, we were blessed with a third son whom we called "Seth," which means "granted," for God had granted me another son for the one Cain killed. After the birth of Seth, I had many, many more sons *and* daughters. I began to see the fulfillment of the name Adam had given me, "Eve", which as I said means "mother of all living." For now I would become the mother of all living. And that is what I have become. Now, all this happened millennia ago.

Imagine my surprise when I saw that I made the cover of *two* of your modern magazines, "Discover" and "Newsweek". One even suggesting that I am your 10,000 great-grandmother. *(walk to table and pick up magazine printouts)* So, in a real sense, you are *all my children.*

Thank you, again, for letting me share my story with you.

NAAMAH

Character: *Naamah (Mrs. Noah)*

Caption: *The "Mother Of All" the second time around*

Publicity Blurb: *"Can you imagine the horror of seeing every person you know, except your husband and children, being drowned by a gigantic flood?"*

Scripture Read: *Genesis 6:5-7; 9:12-16*

Hymns: *"O God, Our Help in Ages Past"*

Scripture Study Prep: *Genesis, Chapters 6 – 9*

Length of Performance: *word count 3,406*

Dress: *blue robe, small head drape*

Shoes: *biblical sandals*

Accessories: *shell jewelry*

Props: *"bow of Colors" made from toy bow from bow and arrow kit. Unstring bow and cover wooden bow with multi-colored cloth and restring; gold letter opener; flute-type recorder; olive sprig; dove from florist; plastic toy domestic food animals, 2 by 2; rectangle whicker chest with lid, approximately 6" x 10" x 13"; with "God's Word" printed on inside*

Make-up: *usual*

Suggested Season to Perform: *Earth Day*

Naamah

The "Mother Of All" The Second Time Around, Mother Of
Shem, Father Of The Semitic People

Hello, my name is Naamah. In my society, a person's name is very important. It is supposed to reflect their character. Well, my name, "Naamah," means "pleasant," "delightful," "sweet." I tried, but I'm not sure I always live up to that.

I come from the noble house of Enoch, firstborn of Cain, who was the first-born of Adam, the father of us all. My family has long been the ruling family in the land of Nod which is located to the east of Eden. My brothers are very famous. Jabal, my half-brother, was the first to domesticate an animal. Now, large herds of livestock graze in our pastures. No longer must we move from place to place in search of meat. Jabal's twin brother, Jubal, is an artist and musician. He not only excels in dance and song, but invented the lyre and the pipe, both of which mysteriously sent music into the air. *((Hold up pipe))* Men come from far away to learn his secrets. As a child, I always wished I could play the lyre, but it was strictly forbidden for women to even touch the magical instrument.

My brother, Tubal-cain, is as inventive as his brothers. He was the first to make utensils and weapons from copper or bronze by burning these special stones in hot, earthen ovens, then hammering the soft metal into useful shapes.

Living in such a famous family, I grew up believing that I was not very important. With brothers like mine, I stood no chance of competing for my father's affection. He was so proud of them. I always wished I could do something that would make him proud of me, but I don't think I ever did. "Naamah", he would say, "you'll never be good for anything but making babies. It's good you have me and your brothers to take care of you."

Yet I must be important to God, for he led me to my husband, Noah. And when the great flood came Noah and I, and our three sons and their wives, were all that were saved.

But I'm getting ahead of my story. When I was growing up, life was good; most people were honest; almost everyone worshiped, or at least tried to follow, what they understood of the God of Adam. But as our cities grew, and our knowledge increased, so did violence. Murders, rapes, and orgies became so common they were not considered news anymore.

The worship of the God of Adam gave way to the perverted worship of man-made gods. It was said that the followers of the Nephilim (fallen gods) offered their virgins to mate with these gods and that this interbreeding was the source of the race of giants who lived in the far north country. I don't know that I believed that story, but that's what was said. My husband was a righteous man and he spoke out against the injustices and evil, but he spoke alone. Even his father and grandfather, who had professed the faith, stood silently by, afraid to witness to the one true God.

One day, Noah came in and told me that while he was in prayer, God spoke to him (I never quite understood how he "heard" from God) and God told him that he had looked down and saw the evil and perversion on the earth. God also said that this saddened him and angered him. He said that he was so angry, he was sorry he had even created "creation." He said that he was going to wipe every living thing (people, animals, even plants) off the face of the earth by a great flood and start all over again.

But God also recognized that Noah was a righteous man. Noah had remained faithful to the teachings of the God of Adam. He had continued to offer sacrifices of penance and thanksgiving and had tried to live in a way in which we held *all* life in reverence — and not only all people, but animals and even plants. All of creation was deemed holy to my husband because it was all created by the great creator.

And so, God revealed to Noah a plan of deliverance. He was to build an enormous boat. God even told him the type of wood to use and gave him a blueprint with the exact dimensions. It would compare to the size of one and a half football fields long, almost the width of a football field, and three stories high. On the top story (around the living quarters) was to be a large open deck, and at one corner, a small enclosed observation tower. Out of curiosity, I asked why it needed to be so big. Then he explained that God had gone on to say that we were to bring a male and a female of every species of animal on earth aboard, as well as many people who believed and desired to flee from the wrath to come.

Well, needless to say, I was skeptical of much of this. First, that God would speak so clearly to a man. Second, we lived many miles from the great waters and very little rain fell in our part of the country. And third, that it would be possible to gather all those animals.

But Noah was convinced that he had heard the voice of God. And so, Noah began building his boat. The work moved slowly. One of the reasons was that our sons were not really "on board" with the project. I think you all know how useless a child is in helping you when they really don't want to be there. Now, my sons were never openly disobedient or even disrespectful to their father. That would simply not be allowed in our culture. But I'm sure that many of you mothers here today can recognize the situation that put me in. I was constantly being caught in the middle.

The boys, (really young men, for all were married but none had children yet) resented their father making them the laughing-stock of town. I think we had all hoped that no one would recognize what Noah was building. After all, who would think of building a boat in our back yard? But this was not to be. Each week, Noah would go to town and stand on the street, preaching end times — preaching that a great flood was coming and that salvation could only come through joining us on the ark that he was building.

For almost a year he labored. I tolerated the building of the ark fairly well, even with the taunting of the neighbors, as long as he used timber from the nearby woods. But when he began dismantling our home because God required gopher wood for a certain section of the boat — and our home was the only source of this wood — I exploded!

"Noah!" I shouted, "now you've gone too far. The ridicule hurts, but I can live with that. But to tear down my house, to tear down the place where our babies were born, where *you* were born, this madness has got to stop!"

28

My husband is a dear, gentle man. He didn't strike me or even shout at me. Instead, he sat me down and we talked almost as equals. He shared with me, deeper than he ever had, his belief in the one true God, the Creator of all that is.

"Honey, I know it sounds like madness to you. But I believe with all my heart that our world is going to be destroyed by water and that this ark is our only hope. Please stand by me. I need you now more than ever."

Well, what do you say when your husband says that? Of course, I agreed to help and "stand by my man". But our children were not as understanding. As I said, they were embarrassed over their father's ludicrous boat sitting out on the dry back yard. They were embarrassed with his street-corner preachings about the end times. They resented being treated as children rather than the adult men that they were. But, after this last conversation with my husband, I set the boys down and explained to them more deeply why we must honor his request. One of the boys asked me if I truly believed that God was going to destroy the world by water. I answered him honestly. I told him that I *did* believe that my *husband* truly believed that the world was going to be destroyed by water, and that was good enough for me. And I persuaded them to humor their father, who was after all, getting on up in years. He would turn six hundred at his next birthday.

The work on the boat went much faster now. And I stepped up my efforts to supply the boat with what we would need for our long sea voyage. My daughters-in-law and I gathered together sleeping pads, clothing, cooking utensils, and food. We gathered nuts, root vegetables, and honeycombs. We collected fruit and fresh vegetables that could be dried. We collected wheat, oats, and barley — all kinds of grains that we could find and ground them up into meal to make into bread. The grains not suitable for human consumption, we collected for the animals. We collected seeds and seedlings for replanting — especially grape seedlings, because it would be very important to have a vineyard soon after we landed. The one food product we did not have to worry about was meat. Though almost everyone else I knew ate meat, Noah had never allowed our family to do so. His reason was that God had never given him permission to eat the flesh of an animal. So we were all vegetarians.

As we worked together, our family became much closer, the way a bond develops when people work together on an important mission. And, you know, I also think it is therapeutic, not only working with wood, but working with wood as father and sons, side-by-side.

As the completion of the ark grew near, I questioned Noah about how he would to go out and collect the animals. His answer was that God would take care of that. And so it happened. Animals, two by two, began just showing up at our place. Soon we had a menagerie in our backyard. I guess you could say we had the first petting zoo. But many of the animals were not the type you would want to pet. I would ask my husband over and over, "Are you sure about the snakes?"

Finally, the fateful day arrived. It was just past midday when the first raindrops began to fall. It seemed like any other summer shower to me. But Noah grew agitated "It is time!" he shouted. "The wrath of God has come! Hurry! Grab your things, and run for the ark! There isn't much time! Boys, help me with the animals!"

Several neighbors heard his shouting and walked over. They stood and jeered. "What's the matter, Noah? Scared of a little rain?" "That madman ought to be locked up," another shouted. "The neighborhood isn't safe with him on the loose."

Noah ignored the taunts. Just as we loaded the last of the supplies and animals aboard, the sky turned dark as night. The rains began to fall in torrents. A wind gust blew down trees and toppled buildings. We watched as the flash floodwaters raced across the sun-hardened earth. Suddenly, the neighbors panicked and began to run in all directions. Noah begged them to come aboard the ark, but they would not.

It was as if the heavens had opened up and all the rain in the heavens poured down on us. And then the ground began to shake. The earth itself opened up and water spewed forth from under the earth. In just minutes the entire area was completely flooded. The ark tossed back and forth upon the waters, bobbing first one way and then another. Finally, the waters settle down and, miraculously, the boat stayed afloat.

It was then that we could hear the screams and cries for help from our neighbors as they beat upon the ark, begging to be taken aboard. But by then, we were helpless to save them. Sometimes, I can still hear their screams. You can't imagine what it's like to witness the death of almost every person you've ever known. I felt no joy in our salvation, only terrible, agonizing grief. In all creation there now remained only myself and Noah and our sons: Ham, Shem, and Japheth, and their wives — eight people in a world totally covered by water.

As soon as we had recovered from the initial shock of the devastation, we set about the work which had to be done. The girls and I began organizing the living and cooking quarters. The men went below to care for the animals.

The rains continued to pour down from heaven incessantly for forty days. I wondered if I would ever see the sun again. Finally, the rains subsided. We all ran upstairs to the observation tower to take a look. But, do you know what we saw? Water! Water! Everywhere! I guess I had thought that we would land as soon as the rains stopped. But that was not the case. The floodwaters still covered the entire earth. There was no place *to* land.

For seven months we floated upon the water. The work of tending the animals was hard, the living accommodations grossly inadequate, the air stuffy and smelly. Yet, I had to admit, there was also a spirit of hope and excitement.

Each morning began with prayers to the great God who had spared our lives. At night, after a difficult day's work, we would gather for a communal meal. Noah would tell the stories of our people, of the beautiful garden and the original mother and father, of Seth and his descendants. He told of Jared and of Enoch, who mysteriously disappeared. Sometimes, I would tell of my ancestors, of Cain and his strange mark, of Jabel and his pet wolf.

Shem would play the lyre and sing sweet ballads. Japheth would play the flute as the rest of the family joined in dance. Before retiring to our sleeping pads, we would once again join in

31

a prayer of thanksgiving for our deliverance. In many ways we were happier than we had ever been.

Then one day as Noah and Japheth were carrying milk from the goats' stalls to feed the lions, the ark shook violently, causing Japheth to spill the milk. We rushed to the living quarters to look out the window and stood together as one by one we realized what had happened. The ark had struck land! The ark was perched upon the highest peak on the Ararat Mountains in the land of Armenia. But still there was no land in sight. For two and a half months, we daily climbed to the observation tower. Always, the result was the same: "Water! Water! Everywhere!"

The high spirits which had sustained us for nine months began to wear thin. Tempers flared. Even the animals grew more restless day by day. Finally, on the first day of the tenth month, the tops of the adjoining mountains could be seen. I have never wanted anything as badly as I wanted to get off that ark. But we had to wait *another six weeks* until one of the birds Noah had sent out returned with an olive branch in its beak — *(hold up olive twig)* proof that life had returned to the earth.

With axes in hand, the men excitedly broke down the door as brilliant sunlight flooded the inner recesses of the ark. Suddenly, trepidation swept over us. As anxious as I had been to set foot on dry land, before us lay a clean, unspoiled new world. We, and all creation, had been given a second chance. And I felt the full weight of that responsibility. Slowly, we descended from the ark. The ground felt firm under our feet. Shem fell on his face and kissed the precious earth.

The first act we did in the new world was to gather stones and build an altar and offer to God a sacrifice of thanksgiving for our great deliverance. As the smoke from the sacrifice rose into the air, I heard the audible voice of God. (Let me tell you, to hear the *audible* voice of God is a very frightening thing). I wrote down his words because I didn't want to be guilty of misquoting him. He said: *(hold up written paper)*

I will never destroy the earth again by flood. As long as the earth endures — seedtime and harvest, cold and heat, summer and winter, day and night — will never cease. Now, be fruitful and multiply and fill the earth. The fear and dread of you will fall on all the beasts of the earth and all the birds of the air, upon every creature that moves along the ground, and upon all fish of the sea. They are given into your hands. Everything that lives and moves will be food for you. Just as I gave you the green plants, now I give you everything.

And then we saw it, those strange lights in the sky. It had begun to rain softly as we were offering our sacrifice and hearing God's voice. The sun was shining through the raindrops, but it was more than that. There were lights of all colors. It looked like fields of brightly colored flowers; first red, then orange, yellow, green, blue, and finally, violet.

"What is it?" one of the girls asked.

"I don't know," I replied. "It's frightening, but it's also beautiful"

Then God began to speak again.

As a sign of my covenant with you, I will set my bow (hold up "bow") the bow with which I sent down the bolts of lightning and rain — I will set my rainbow down and every time the rain clouds gather, I will see my rainbow of many colors — and will remember my covenant with you.

Go and teach others of my great love for you and of the rules you must follow.

Did God mean to destroy all but the eight of us? Did he give his warning to others? Was my Noah simply the only man on earth to hear and heed God's words? I guess I'll never know for sure.

But I do know this: If you honor God, God will honor you. My family is living proof.

Thank you.

SARAH

Character: *Sarah*

Caption: *The World's Oldest First-time Mother*

Publicity Blurb: *"Can you imagine my reaction when my husband told me that he came within inches of killing my precious son in some bizarre human sacrifice?"*

Scripture: *Genesis 21:1-3*

Hymns: *"Trust and Obey"*

Scripture Study Prep: *Genesis, Chapters 17 – 22*

Length of Performance: *word count 2,756*

Dress: *brown robe, head drape*

Shoes: *biblical sandals*

Accessories: *Egyptian jewelry*

Props: *wooden walking stick, reprint of floor plan of Abraham's possible home in Ur, available on-line @ plans of a private home in Ur of the Chaldeans at the time of Abraham; (floor plan ran on front page of New York Times in the 1920's)*

Make-up: *heavy eyeliner, green eye shadow*

Suggested Season to Perform: *any time*

Sarah

The Oldest First Time Mother,
Mother Of Isaac, The Child Of Promise

Hello, my name is Sarai. I know you know me as Sarah, but I lived most of my life as Sarai, until God changed the name. I grew up in the bustling city of Ur, in your present land of Iraq. My father was the renowned idol-maker Terah. As a very young girl, I was enamored with my older half-brother, Abram.

As a young woman, my dreams came true when Abram asked me to be his wife. We were happy together, but no babies were born. My prayers for a child increased as the years increased. You see, my religion taught that a barren woman cannot enter heaven.

One day when Abram came in from tending the sheep, I could see a difference on his face.

"Sarai," he said, "God has spoken to me."

"Which God?" I asked, for we had many.

"I don't really know," my husband admitted. "All I know is that some god spoke to me. He told me to gather my family and move to a land far from here, a land he would show me. And there, Sarai, he promised to make me the father of many nations. I have to go, Sarai. *You* have to go. My father, my nephew Lot, all of us in this household must do as God has commanded."

I didn't want to leave. It was crazy. I loved the hustle and bustle of the city. You see, the city of Ur was on the major trade route to India. Caravans came through daily with goods from all over the world. And, I loved the comforts of a well-built and well-staffed home. Our home was one of the finest in Ur; over three thousand square feet. There's a blueprint of our home over on that table. I can't say for sure that it is a print of our home, but certainly one of a house in our neighborhood. And, I understand that a copy of that blueprint appeared on the front page of your *New York Times* back in the 1920s.

We even had indoor plumbing. The toilet had a pit lined with ceramic rings covered in bitumen (tar) with a baked brick drainage pipe which emptied into a deep pit in the backyard, which was covered over with earth from time to time. The top of the pit had an attractive ceramic "seat" similar to yours. A large pottery container of water set nearby. After usage, one had only to scoop up a bucket of water and pour it down the pit.

My "facility" even had a large washing tub, large enough to not only sit, but recline in pleasure. The bathing tub also had a similar drainage pipe. Of course, the water had to be poured in from the large water storage holder which, in turn, had to be refilled from either the decorative cistern in the courtyard or one of the two larger ones in the rear of the property. Hard work, yes. But what are servants for?

So, I think you can see why I had no desire to head out on a journey to goodness knows where, living in tents, traveling in the dust of herds of sheep, herds of goats, camels, oxen. But he was my husband and I had promised to go where he went. I knew I had no choice.

So, we packed up all our possessions and left. Our father was old and in poor health, so we stopped in the city of Haran, in the country you call Turkey, and lived there until Terah died. I did not enjoy Haran as much as I had Ur. My home was not as nice as the one in Ur, but it was all right.

I was 65 years old and Abram was 75. Haran was as good a place as any to live out our remaining years. Then one day Abram came in and I could see by the look on his face that his God had spoken to him again.

"Sarai", he said, "God has spoken to me."

"Which god?" I asked again.

"I still don't know exactly", he admitted. "But God told me to gather my family and move to the land not too far from here, a land he would show me. And there, Sarai, he promised again to make me the father of many nations! Sarai, we must go. We have to go!"

"Abram", I said, "you're crazy." And I walked out of the house.

But, he was my husband and I had promised to go where he went. I knew I had no choice. So, once again, Abram went forth, wandering, waiting for his god to reveal the land that would be his and his descendants forever. We packed up all our possessions and leaving Haran, we moved south along the River Balikn for seventy miles. There, we picked up the major caravan route which connected the countries of Sumer and Egypt. We traveled to the west for about one hundred miles.

We arrived at a village in the present day country of Syria, which was in distress. We found a stricken city, no longer bustling with trade. The town had fallen victim to the unpredictable weather of the region. For months, there had been no rain. The streams had dried up, crops had failed. As the grass and grain withered away, the cows were no longer able to give milk. Families were forced to butcher their dairy cows and goats in order to have food to eat. By the time we arrived, the people were sick and malnourished, with the tell-tale signs of bloated stomachs. Other caravans had passed through this area during the famine, but had hurried on their way.

Just as we arrived, the rains returned. The people could recognize Abram as a great religious leader and they attributed the rains to his presence. When my husband saw the suffering of the people, he had compassion. He ordered our men to set up camp in a field on the outskirts of the city. Immediately, a system of dispensing grain, meat, herbs and what medicines we had was set up. Additional men were assigned to our clan's healer and the townspeople streamed to him for help.

To replenish the calcium which was deficient in the people, Abram ordered each family in our clan to donate fresh milk. As an example to our people, he publicly milked the prize cow of our own herd. This cow was unique in that she was snow white, without any coloring or marking.

Being a superstitious people, the townspeople attached a deep religious significance to the "white cow", believing her milk to possess magical healing properties. The recovery of the people was remarkable. Within three weeks, most of the people were well again. Abram bartered with them, allowing the townspeople to obtain a starter herd of cattle and sheep while retaining their dignity. When our caravan left, heading south for Damascus, roughly two hundred miles away, the prayers of the people went with us.

To honor this great gift of Abram, the people named their town Halab Shahba, which in Arabic means "to milk the white cow". This city is still inhabited today, and goes by the name of Aleppo, which is once again devastated with its people suffering.

Continuing to journey south, with all our possessions, finally we reached the land of Canaan and God revealed that this was to be our promised land. Once there, I assumed Abram would settle down and provide me with a beautiful home, as befitting our great wealth. But did he? No! We continued to live in goat-hair tents, wandering as poor nomads — so much so that he acquired the name of a "wandering Aramean." Oh, how I missed the luxury of a *bathtub*!

As we wandered in the land of Canaan, famine fell over the land, forcing us further and further south in search of adequate grazing for our many herds. Finally, we reached the country of Egypt and civilization again. We stood in awe before the eight hundred year old pyramids of Giza.

Abram had told me that because I was so beautiful, he was afraid the Pharaoh would want me for himself and kill Abram for me. I knew I was very beautiful, but I seriously doubted that the Pharaoh would take such a drastic action. But Abram was adamant that this was a good plan. He had already spread the word that I was his sister, not his wife. Of course, that was half true. Abram was my half-brother. I didn't like the deception, but I did enjoy life along the Nile. My days were filled with browsing and buying in some of the finest shops and bazaars in the world.

Then one day while Abram was away, Pharaoh's men came and took me away to the palace to become part of the royal harem. As soon as Abram returned and found out what happened, he rushed to the palace, making a full confession to the Pharaoh, explaining his weird reason. The Pharaoh was furious. In the Egyptian culture, adultery was a crime punishable by death. He ordered us out of the palace and out of the country. And, he gave great gifts to hurry us on our way. We were actually wealthier when we left Egypt than when we entered. So maybe Abram's plan wasn't too bad after all.

Over the next many years, I watched my husband struggle with the unfulfilled promise of his God. I was well beyond childbearing age, yet Abram still clung to the promise of "someday, some day." I tried to help. I suggested that he adopt Eliezer, who had been his trusted servant ever since Eliezer was a young boy and the idea sounded good to Abram. But, when he asked God about it, God said "No," that the child of promise would come from (as God put it) Abram's own bowels. God even elaborated on his original promise. "As the stars cover the night sky, Abram," he said, "so numerous shall your seed be."

But still there was no child. Then, I had another idea. I could "loan" my handmaiden Hagar to my husband. If she conceived, then my Abram would have his son. I mentioned the idea to Abram and he readily agreed — a little *too* readily. Hagar accomplished in one evening what I had not been able to accomplish in sixty years. She became pregnant.

Suddenly, my sweet, docile servant girl became a haughty shrew. She wouldn't obey me half the time and when she did, she did so arrogantly. I began to discipline her and she ran away. Abram was concerned, but in a few days she returned — a great deal more humble.

She and I existed side-by-side in an uneasy alliance until the birth of her son. Then, something happened that I had not counted on. I knew little Ishmael would become the most important thing in Abram's life. What I hadn't counted on was how important that would make his mother.

Twelve years later, Abram had another message from his God. I was in the tent when I heard Abram talking to several men. I looked out and saw three strange men. Abram was carrying on an animated conversation with one of them. Suddenly, Abram ran into the tent and ordered me to go instruct one of the servants to kill and slaughter a fattened calf and bring it to me. I was to roast the beef and make some flat bread to go with it to serve his guests.

I did as I was told and while I was cooking, I leaned my ear close to the tent opening so that I could listen to the conversation. Abram and one of the men were discussing the destruction of the cities of Sodom and Gomorrah. Then I heard Abram say, "And you say that my Sarai will bear a son?"

I laughed out loud. I couldn't help myself. Sure, a ninety year old woman is going to have a baby! Then, I heard the man say, "Why do you laugh, Sarai? Is anything too hard for God? I tell you that this time next year you will bring forth from your womb, a son. From this time forth, Sarai, your name shall be *Sarah*, for you shall be the mother of kings. And your husband, Abram, shall be called *Abraham*, for he shall be the father of many nations."

I didn't know who the man was, but he spoke with such authority I was not inclined to argue with him. Yet, I couldn't believe his words. But would you believe that exactly one year later, I gave birth to a precious baby boy! I named him *Isaac*, which means "laughter" because I had laughed when the man, or the messenger, had spoken, and I've been laughing ever since.

On the day of the celebration of Isaac's weaning, I looked up and saw the haughty face of Hagar. Suddenly, I couldn't take it any longer. In a fury, I banished her and her son from our camp. Abraham pleaded with me to change my mind for he had grown terribly fond Ishmael. But my mind was made up. Abraham went to God, telling on me, trying to get God to take his side.

But God didn't. God told Abraham that I was right. Abraham knew he couldn't fight both of us, so he stood by as I drove Hagar and Ishmael out of camp. I've never been sorry I did that.

My life was much happier with them gone. But I still didn't have a home made of brick and mortar. Abraham insisted on living a nomadic life. I finally quit asking him to change and resigned myself to being a sheepherder's wife. I had my Isaac. My whole life revolved around him.

Then one day when Isaac was a young man, he and his father left secretly in the middle of the night and were gone for several days. None of the servants seemed to know where they had gone. When they returned, neither would tell me anything except that God had required the trip — it was some sort of test.

I couldn't get any more out of them, but it was plain that something dramatic had happened. Abraham had taken my youngster off and brought him back to me a man. And Abraham had changed also. He was quieter spoken, softer with me. It was several years later, before Abraham told me the whole story. God

40

had told him to take Isaac and climb Mt. Moriah and there offer a sacrifice.

When they arrived at the place, God told Abraham that the sacrifice was to be our son, my *only* son Isaac! Abraham said that he cried and pleaded with God, but finally bound Isaac to the altar and raised his knife to murder my son! At the last minute, God spoke and released Abraham from the terrible deed, supplying a ram caught in a thicket as a substitute sacrifice. God, he said, was testing his faith.

Well, you can imagine how I reacted. I let my husband know, in no uncertain terms, that I didn't care *what* his God said. He had better never do anything to harm my son again! If he did, he would have *me* to answer to. And if he feared the wrath of his God, that was *nothing* compared to the wrath I could wield.

Since that time, my son, and his son Jacob, and Jacob's twelve sons have gone on to create a great dynasty. Truly, I have become the mother of kings. And eventually, I did become a believer in Abraham's God. It takes some of us longer than others, I guess. But, fortunately, I *have* learned a little in my old age.

One thing I've learned is that so often it looks like God isn't doing so good, is taking too long, and needs a little help. I still think a person *should do* what they can. But, in the final analysis, God really *is* able to do that which he has promised.

Our job, and it is still a hard one for me, is to trust — to trust and obey. For there is no other way to be happy with our God, but to trust and obey.

Thank you for letting me come and share my thoughts with you...

LEAH

Character: *Leah*

Caption: *the lesser-loved wife*

Publicity Blurb: *"Can you imagine what it feels like to spend your honeymoon night with a husband so drunk he thinks you are your sister?"*

Scripture: *Genesis 29: 31,35a*

Hymns: *"God Will Take Care Of You"*

Scripture Study Prep: *Genesis, Chapters 29 – 30, Chapter 35:16-18*

Length of Performance: *word count 2,756*

Dress: *brown robe, head drape*

Shoes: *biblical sandals*

Accessories: *Egyptian necklace;*

Props: *nose ring, small gold clip-on earring will do; card with all Jacob's children and by whom*

Make-up: *heavy eye liner and green eye shadow*

Suggested Season to Perform: *no special time*

Leah

The Lesser-Loved Wife, The Mother Of Judah

Hello, my name is Leah, daughter of Laban of Paddanaram. My name means "weary" and I'm afraid most of my life reflects this mood. My grandfather is Nahor, brother to our leader Abraham. My aunt, Rebecca, is married to Isaac, son of Abraham. So you can see I come from a very honorable family.

One day, Jacob, son of Isaac and Aunt Rebecca, came to our land. Rachel, my younger sister, saw him first while she was tending the sheep. She came rushing home to tell us of Jacob's presence. My father was overjoyed with meeting a relative, especially the grandson of the revered Abraham. Though usually quite stingy, he treated Jacob as royalty.

For a month, Jacob lived with us as our guest and occasionally worked in the fields. Though Rachel was still only a child, it was obvious to see the immediate affection Jacob and Rachel had for one another. Each evening, Rachel would climb up into cousin Jacob's lap as stories were told. It just didn't seem proper to me. My sister is a very sweet and beautiful girl, but I felt that at almost ten years of age she should behave as a young woman, not as a child. Father never seemed to mind what I considered over-familiarity. And so against my better judgment, the fondness was permitted to grow.

I was not jealous, though I'm sure that's what everyone thought. You see, I was a little past marrying age, but no one had asked for my hand in marriage yet. People made fun of me behind my back. My eyes are weak and I have to squint so that I can see. But I am a hard worker and I love to cook, sew, and care for babies. I knew I would make some man a wonderful wife. Well, after Jacob had stayed with us for over a month, Father said to Jacob, "My kinsman, it is not right for you to work here for me and for no pay. What wages shall I pay you?"

Jacob replied that the only wages he wanted was the hand of Rachel in marriage. "You know she is still too young to be given to a man," responded Father. "I'll tell you what I will do. If you will work for me for seven years, then Rachel will be yours."

Jacob became an integral part of our family, entertaining us with accounts of his many exploits. He was always courteous to me, though it was obvious to everyone that his heart belonged to Rachel.

The seven years went by fast. Rachel grew up into the beautiful, desirable woman I knew she would. At seventeen years, she was ready to be given in marriage, and Jacob had fulfilled his contract. The time came for the wedding celebration. Jacob was happier than I'd ever seen him, and Rachel literally glowed.

Something had been bothering me for years, but since Father never mentioned it, neither had I. That was that I was not married. I understood why no man would want to marry me, but I didn't quite see how Rachel could get married before I did.

When I finally asked Father about it, he didn't seem to see this as a problem. "Don't worry," he said. "I have it all worked out. You will be married before she is. Trust me."

As the wedding day grew near, one could tell the mounting excitement in Jacob. Rachel sang as she did her chores. Love is so wonderful, I thought.

I helped Rachel pack her dowry chest and work on her wedding dress. Father had allowed her to buy some very expensive lace and some small seashells from a passing caravan. The lace and small shells transformed the dress into a gown fit for a princess. Rachel and I giggled as young girls as we labor to bring everything to perfection. I reworked a dress I had so that it would do for my wedding. I didn't expect my ceremony would be much of an affair.

I tried to stay upbeat. But, when I was away from Rachel, my mind was troubled. The wedding was only days away, and still I was unmarried. Again, I questioned Father. "What are we going to do about my singleness?" I asked. "I do not want to cause my sister any sadness."

"I told you not to worry," he replied, seemingly agitated that I had brought up the matter again. "I have taken care of everything! Trust me!"

Perhaps, I thought, he has secured a husband for me, and we will be married just prior to Rachel's wedding. Maybe, he wasn't telling me because he feared I would object to the man he had selected. Father needn't have worried. I would never do anything to hurt my sister, and besides, Father wouldn't listen to any objection I had anyway.

The remaining days passed and the hour of the wedding celebration grew near and still there was no man for me. Father called me aside. I feared that his plans had grown awry. "Oh, poor Rachel," I thought. If his plan for me had fallen through, then Rachel couldn't marry her beloved Jacob.

"It's time now," Father said to me, "to put my plan into action."

"Oh, really," I sighed in relief. "Where is the man you have picked for me?" I scanned the crowd looking for the potential bridegroom.

"It's Jacob," he replied curtly.

"What do you mean? Jacob is to be married to Rachel. You know of their great love."

"No. You are to put on Rachel's wedding dress and heavy veil."

Rachel overheard his statement. She and I looked at each other in total disbelief. Neither of us could believe our father.

"He'll marry you first. Then, he can have Rachel later," he bellowed as he left the room.

"No!" I cried.

"No! No!" screamed Rachel amidst a flood of tears.

But Father's mind was made up. Not many people knew my father for the kind of man he really was. He was heartless and cruel. But this cruelty surprised even me. We had no choice. Father ruled us with an iron fist. We had no choice in the matter.

Without words, Rachel and I undressed, and I put on her wedding dress and the heavy veil. Rachel put back on her own clothes. We embraced awkwardly. Then, she left to hide and empty her grief alone.

I had to walk beside Father to the place of the ceremony. By the time we arrived, the men had been drinking for days. Jacob looked at me with love in his eyes, but I could tell that he could not see through the veil. He had no idea that I was not his beloved Rachel.

The ceremony was short. Jacob went back immediately to celebrate with the men and I went to the wedding chamber alone. At nightfall, Jacob came to the room. I had not lighted any candles, but was sitting solemnly in the chair in the dark, still in my wedding clothes.

"My wife!" he cried out, "Where are you?"

"I am here, my husband," I replied as I rose and started to light the lamp.

"No need for light tonight, my little one," he said. He held me tightly, lifted my veil and kissed me. Then, in his drunkenness, hurriedly undressed me and consummated our marriage, all the while saying, "Oh, Rachel, Rachel, my Rachel!"

Do you have any idea what it is like to spend your honeymoon night with a man so drunk that he thinks he has just married your sister, who thinks he is making love to his beloved? I was thankful that the heavy drinking caused him to go to sleep very quickly.

I lay in the bed with tears streaming down my face. Oh, it would have been my choice to have never married, even with the curse of banishment from heaven, than to have married like this. Finally, I drifted off to uneasy sleep.

Toward day, Jacob began to stir. My back was to him and he playfully cuddled me. "Oh, Rachel, my bride," he said as he turned me over in the bed. I will never forget the look on his face. "Leah! What are you doing here?" he screamed. "Get out of my bed! Where is Rachel?"

I had to tell him what Father had done; that Father had tricked him into marrying me first, that Father had purposely gotten him so drunk that he didn't know the difference between us in the dark.

I've never seen anyone more angry than Jacob. Murder was in his eyes. He grabbed his robe and hurried out of the room. I truly feared for my father's life.

When Jacob found Father in the fields, it took three men to restrain Jacob as he sought to tear Father apart with his bare hands.

"It's our custom that the older daughter marry first," curtly replied Father. "I'm surprised you didn't know that."

Jacob, who was quite a trickster himself, realized that he had been tricked by the master trickster. But the marriage had been consummated. I was Jacob's wife. There was literally nothing he could do. He had been outwitted fair and square.

Father, with a smirk on his face, continued, "If you want Rachel so much, work seven years for her like you did for Leah."

"Another seven years before I have Rachel! You can't mean that!"

"I tell you what I'll do," offered Father. "Go ahead with the week-long wedding celebration with Leah and at the end of the week you can marry Rachel. But you'll have to promise to work for me seven years in payment of Rachel. That's the deal. Take it or leave it."

Jacob loved Rachel enough to work those first seven years for her. He loved her enough to work a second seven years. Fourteen years for one woman! He loved Rachel enough to be married to me. And so, with his head hanging, he returned to the bedroom and told me of his decision.

We spent the week together, our honeymoon week. We made love a few times, but I knew that Rachel would always have his heart.

Yet, God looked with kindness upon me. In the years to come, I was the one who bore the first four sons unto Jacob. In my culture, a person's name is very important. It makes a statement about how the mother feels about her child. So, I was careful in the way I named my children, as was Rachel.[7]

Forgive me for consulting my notes. But, when you get to be as old as I am, you have to write things down.

I named my first son Reuben, meaning "God has noticed my trouble", for I said, "Jehovah has noticed my trouble — now my husband will love me." I quickly became pregnant again, and I named my second son Simeon, meaning "Jehovah heard", for I said, "Jehovah heard that I was unloved and he has given me another son." I became pregnant a third time and I named that son Levi, which means "attachment", for I said, "Surely now my husband will feel affection for me, since I have given him three

7 Genesis 29:31-35, 35:18 (NRSV)

sons!" And, for a fourth time, I conceived and bore a son whom I named Judah, meaning "praise", for now I was truly praising Jehovah.

During all this time, Rachel remained barren. In desperation, Rachel gave her slave girl, Bilhab, to Jacob, and she bore Jacob two sons. The first son, Rachel named Dan, which means "justice," for she said, "God has given me justice and heard my plea." The second son by Bilhad, she named Naphtali, which means "wrestling." for she said, "I am in a fierce contest with my sister and I am winning!"

After the birth of those two boys, I realized I wasn't getting pregnant anymore. So, I gave Jacob my slave girl, Zilpah, who also bore him two sons. The first son I named Gad, meaning "My luck has turned!" The second child by Zilpah, I named Asher, meaning "happy," for I said, "What joy is mine! The other women will think me blessed indeed!"

Jacob didn't visit my bed too often in those days. One day my oldest son, Reuben, brought me some mandrake plants he had found growing nearby. Mandrakes were highly prized in our culture because, not only were they a powerful aphrodisiac, they were also believed to promote conception. Rachel saw Reuben give me the mandrakes and begged me for them.

"Isn't it enough that you have taken my husband, for I never see him anymore," I said. "Now you want my son's mandrake plants as well?"

But Rachel offered Jacob to me for the night in exchange for the plants and I agreed. Well, the mandrakes didn't do her any good. She still didn't conceive.

But I did! Three more times! The first son of this set, I named Issachar, which means "wages," for I said, "God has repaid me for giving my slave-girl to my husband for a price." The next son I named Zebulum, meaning "gifts," for I said, "God has given me good gifts for my husband. Now he will honor me, for I have given him six sons." I conceived once more and God blessed me with a precious little girl, whom I named Dinah.

Six sons and one daughter, and still Rachel was barren. Finally, God took pity on Rachel and answered her prayers. He opened the womb of Rachel and she bore Jacob a son, Joseph, which means "May I also have another!" Then years later, she bore a second son, but she died in childbirth. With her last breath, she named him Ben-oni, meaning "son of my sorrow." But Jacob couldn't bear that name, so he renamed the child Benjamin, meaning "son of my right hand."

I never had Jacob's special love. I could never compete with Rachel for that. But I was a good wife and a good friend to Jacob. I managed his household well. I raised his twelve sons and watched them become respected leaders.

Through tricked by his brothers, Rachel's son Joseph ultimately became prime minister of Egypt. In our old age, our whole clan moved to Egypt to be near him.

Jacob was a good husband to me, far better than I would have ever believed possible. I have had wealth, prestige, and a place of belonging. God's promise to Abraham, Isaac, and Jacob was fulfilled through me. My son Levi's descendants became the tribe of priests. And, my son Judah became an ancestor to King David, the greatest king of Israel, and, eventually, ancestor of our Lord Jesus Christ. Not a bad legacy for a weak-eyed old maid.

The saying is true that all things work together for good for those who love God.

RAHAB

Character: *Rahab*

Caption: *Head Madam Of Jericho; Mother-In-Law Of Ruth*

Publicity Blurb: *"Can you imagine what it is like to see your hometown and everyone in it destroyed and know that you are the one who befriended the enemy?"*

Scripture: *Joshua 6:25*

Hymns: *"Something Beautiful"*

Scripture Study Prep: *Joshua, Chapters 2 – 6*

Length of Performance: *word count 3,012*

Dress: *blue robe, brightly colored head drape*

Shoes: *gold sandals*

Accessories: *large, gaudy jewelry*

Props: *none*

Make-up: *heavy "painted" face*

Suggested Season to Perform: *no special time*

Rahab

Head Madam Of Jericho, Mother Of Boaz, Mother-In-Law Of Ruth

Hello, my name is Rahab. I'm sure most of you have heard of me. And most of you probably don't think much of me. But I would still like to share my story with you.

I was born and raised in the exciting city of Jericho. As a child, I was fascinated by the ancient ruins which lay just to the east of the city. Some people say that Jericho is the oldest continuously inhabited city in the world. I don't know about that. But I did grow up spending hours sifting through the layered rubble of past lives.

I loved my city, but I didn't like the poverty I experienced. I resolved never to be poor when I grew up.

In my society there were few careers open to poor, untrained women. But there was one profession which required not money but good looks; not education but personality. It was the oldest profession known to man, or should I say, known to woman — prostitution. I chose this way of life to achieve fame and fortune, and therefore, happiness.

I was good at my job. In only three years I became the leading prostitute in Jericho. I was able to purchase a house with a courtyard and a separate apartment. I was able to fill my home with the finest furnishings. I now had money and possessions. I had arrived at my goal. And yet, I had not found happiness.

I had worshiped a pantheon of gods, El, the King, also known as the Bull, Baal, the god of fertility; the mother-goddesses, Anath, Asherah, Astarte, and the moon god Jerach. But I had never found any joy or solace in their teachings.

Then, I heard about a god who had freed thousands of people from slavery in Egypt. These people, it was said, were now living in the desert east of us. Some townspeople feared attack from these strange Hebrews. Others said they had lived in our land hundreds of years before and that their god was leading them back to reclaim this land.

It was all very confusing to me. If their god, whom they called Yahweh, was powerful enough to free them from Pharaoh's grasp, then surely this god could give them the victory over the land of Canaan.

I understood why many people were fearful. Jericho stood at the entrance of the country. If there was to be an invasion, it would logically be here. Yet, Jericho was defended by only one battalion of soldiers.

I was not without fear myself, but I was extremely curious. Why would their god grant a powerful victory, only to leave the people wandering aimlessly in the wilderness, for it had been forty years since the historic escape from Egypt? And yet, they didn't seem to be abandoned by their god, either. Reports of minor skirmishes with nomadic tribes told of almost magical military victories by these Hebrews.

Even more difficult to understand were reports of what their god required of them. There were no human sacrifices, no self-mutilations, no sex orgies. Their god taught the value of human life; thou shalt not kill, thou shalt not steal, thou shalt not commit adultery or lie or covet. This god was a god of love, of joy, of compassion, of second chances.

I wanted desperately to learn more. Would this god accept me? Could I experience love? In spite of my profession, I had never really known love from anyone but my parents. I wanted to know more about this god. And I wanted to know people who respected one another as their normal way of life.

But these people never visited our city. There was no way for me to meet a follower of Yahweh. I was trapped into my way of life, a way of life which now seemed cheaper and dirtier as the years went by.

One day a knock came at my door. When I opened the door, two strangers hurried in, locking the door behind them. "Please, we need shelter for the night. May we sleep here?" anxiously asked one of the men.

This request was original, to say the least. Lodging was not the service I was accustomed to providing. The men's appearance was as odd as their behavior. Their dress was not the common dress of Jericho or of the visitors who frequented our city. And though they spoke our language, it was with a heavy, unfamiliar accent. I began to feel uneasy. Something was not right. How could I tactfully ask these strangers to leave?

Suddenly, there was a pounding at the door. "Open up, Rahab, in the name of the king."

As I started for the door, one of the strangers grabbed my arm. "Please," he pleaded, "help us. We are the ones they are searching for."

As I looked into the man's face, I was surprised by the absence of fear in his eyes. There was concern certainly, but there was also kindness and integrity. I felt I could trust this man with my life. I'm not sure where I found the courage to take such a chance, but I instantly agreed to help the men.

"Just a minute, "I shouted through the locked door. "I don't have on any clothes."

"When did that ever matter to you?" shouted back one of the soldiers.

Quickly, I led the strangers through my house and up the ladder to the roof. "Hurry, hide under the flax over in the corner. And, for goodness sake, keep still and quiet." I hurried down the ladder, through the house, and opened the front door.

"Okay, Rahab, where are they," said the captain as he and two other officers pushed their way inside.

"Where are who?" I innocently replied.

"You know who we mean, the Hebrew spies. Your neighbor said that two strange men entered your house a few minutes ago."

"Captain, many men enter my house in a day and some are rather strange. However, at present I am alone. If my neighbor had continued to spy on me, she would have seen the two men leave immediately. They were only making appointments for future visits. The last time I saw them, they were leaving town through the city gates. If your men hurry, they could probably overtake them with ease. Now, that's enough business. Please sit down and let me serve you a cool drink."

"Rahab. This is not a social visit. It is imperative that we find these men. The safety of the city is at stake."

The captain called for three soldiers to search my home while the rest of the company hurried out of the city in search of the dangerous spies.

Well, the soldiers searched my house and the apartment, but found no one. Then, the captain and his men hurried on to catch up with the others.

"Oh, Rahab," I thought, "what have you gone and done?" If anyone ever found out that I had aided the spies, by career would be over and possibly my life, as well.

After I was sure the soldiers were gone, I climbed the ladder and called to the spies. "You can come out now, the soldiers have gone. Come into the house quickly before my nosy neighbor sees you."

When they were safely inside I began my questions. "Why did you come to my house?"

"Our God, Yahweh, guided us to this home," answered the taller stranger.

"Then, you are the Hebrews, the followers of Yahweh!" I exclaimed excitedly.

"How do you know of Yahweh?" asked the stranger with the kind eyes.

"Everyone in Jericho has heard of your god and of what he did for you in Egypt. Everyone in Jericho fears you and your god."

"Then, why did you protect us?"

"I didn't know for sure that you were followers of this Yahweh. But I did feel that you would not harm me. I'm glad I helped you for I have wanted to learn about your god. Do you think that your god would accept me?"

"I'm sure He would. But this is really not the time to discuss religion. We must get out of the city. Can you help us escape?"

"I'll help you escape," I said, "if you promise that when your god destroys Jericho, I and my household, my parents, my brothers, and my servants will be spared."

The Hebrews agreed and instructed me to hang a red cord from my window on the day of battle so that when the fighting began, the soldiers would know not to enter my house.

While we waited for darkness, I served the men food and was able to question them further about this strange new God, Yahweh. When darkness fell, I opened my bedroom window, tied a heavy rope to my bedpost, and lowered the men to safety over the city wall. As the second man made ready to climb down, I made a causal remark, "You were lucky to choose my house. Not many homes are built into the city wall."

"You might call it luck," he replied with a twinkle in his eyes, "but I call it God."

Quickly, the men descended the rope and rushed for cover. I pulled the rope up after them and sat down upon my bed to contemplate the events of the last few hours.

The next morning, I explained the situation to my family. Later in the day, I went to the marketplace and bought up all the red cords and red material I could find. Three days later, an alarm sounded throughout the city that the Hebrews had arrived at the River Jordan. The city gates were quickly locked and barred. Everyone was on heightened alert. Three days after that, the alarm sounded again. The Hebrews had now crossed the River Jordan and were camped just over a mile from town. I hurriedly hung red cords from all my windows and prayed. I gave strict instructions to everyone in my house not to go outdoors, no matter what! My younger brothers protested, but since I paid the bills, they obeyed.

For three days, we sat inside my house and waited. And nothing happened! And then, the Hebrews began to march on the city. From my bedroom window, I saw the strangest sight. The Hebrews were strung out in a line over three miles long. First, came twenty thousand soldiers armed for battle. Seven priests blowing seven trumpets of rams' horns followed the soldiers. Following the priests was a small box measuring four by two foot attached to long poles and carried by four men. The box was covered completely in gold which glistened in the sun. The priests and attendants were elaborately dressed, their jewels also catching the sun's rays. Twenty thousand soldiers brought up the rear. (Maybe, my numbers are off, but it was an awful lot of men.) "It will all be over soon," I said to my family. "Now you will see the power of Yahweh."

Imagine my surprise and my disappointment when nothing happened. The Hebrews simply marched around the city, the seven priests loudly blowing their trumpets. Then, they returned to their camp. From my window I could hear the jeers of the townspeople, but our gates stayed locked. The next day, the Hebrews did the same thing. For six days they appeared, blew their trumpets, marched, and retreated, as we sat huddled in my home.

My brothers were impatient to leave the house and join their friends in taunts. Then, on the seventh day, the Hebrews marched again. But this time when they had circled the city once blowing their trumpets, they circled it again, and again. As they completed their circle the seventh time, Joshua, their leader, gave a command to let out a great shout. In one accord all forty thousand people shouted in a tremendous voice, "Praise be to Yahweh! Mighty is he! Walls of stone, tumble down, says he!"

Then, I felt it. The ground began to shake. My bedroom wall swayed slightly. From my window I could see the city wall all around me begin to crumble. "Oh, Yahweh," I cried, "protect me as your followers have promised." Quickly, we threw out the red material and cords from *every* window. My house virtually glowed red in the brilliant sun. I guess my house was the first red light district.

The destruction around me continued to increase, but my walls held firm. We could hear the sound of warfare as the Hebrew soldiers climbed over the rubble which had been our mighty fortress and engaged the Canaanite defenders. We could hear the clash of swords, the screams of women and children. We were completely at the mercy of the Hebrews and their God.

The noise of the battle ceased and still we sat huddled in the living area of my home. "Yahweh will protect us," I kept promising my family, hoping that if I said it often enough I would believe it myself. Then, we heard a knock at our door. My mother panicked, but I reasoned that soldiers coming to kill us would not bother to knock.

Bravely, I opened the door. There stood the two strangers I had befriended. "Quick, gather your possessions. We are about to burn the city."

My family left with only the possessions we could carry on our backs. "Where are the prisoners?" I asked as we hurried through the destroyed city, stepping over the slain men and women and children.

"There are no prisoners," dispassionately answered our new friend. "Yahweh demanded that all the inhabitants of the city be killed."

A shutter went through me. "What, indeed, have I gotten myself into? What happened to Yahweh, God of love and compassion? I have much to learn about this new God."

But I had made my decision. My lot had been cast. The people of Jericho were gone forever. I had no choice but to go forward. I did not look back as my prized home went up in smoke.

Just before we crossed back over the river, the people slowed their pace as they gazed at a pile of stones. "What's happening?" I asked. "What's so special about a pile of rocks?" It was explained to me that this *pile of rocks* was a sacred site, a monument of remembrance, commemorating the miracle God had performed by stopping the River Jordan so the people could cross over on dry ground.

The days and weeks which followed were awkward for me and my family. The Hebrew leader, Joshua, had officially accepted us into his clan, but we were shunned by the people. We weren't mistreated, but we were clearly considered not good enough to be accepted by these God-fearing people. I thought, perhaps, that it was because of my former occupation. One day, I asked an older woman who had slightly befriended me if I was being shunned because I had been a harlot.

"Goodness, no!" she replied. "We would never do that. It's because you and your people are heathens."

"What do you mean *heathen*?" I asked.

She looked at me as though I was a simpleton. "Because you don't follow the teaching of Yahweh," she answered curtly.

"But I've never been taught the teaching of Yahweh," I answered in defense. "I had never even met anyone who served him until the spies came to my house."

"Well, we just don't like to associate with folks who don't believe the way we do."

"How do I learn?" I asked.

She shrugged her shoulders and walked away.

It looked as though my family and I would have to leave this group and try to find a Canaanite village which would take us in. But Yahweh had a better plan.

A man named Salmon came to my tent one day and asked if I would consent to marry him. I had seen him around camp, but had never even spoken to him before. "Why would you want me?" I asked. "Don't you consider me a pagan heathen like everyone else does?"

"Rahab, I believe you possess the strongest faith of anyone in camp," he replied. "You trusted Yahweh with your life. I admire your bravery, your courage, and your strength. And, you are also a very beautiful woman. Will you consent to be my wife?"

"You know the life I led in Jericho," I said. "I was a prostitute. Could you accept me as your wife knowing how I earned my living? Could you accept me just as I am?"

"Yahweh is giving us all a new beginning if only we will accept it," he replied.

"Then my answer to you is *yes*", I said. "With you and your god — no with *my* God, I will begin my life anew."

When much of the fighting was over and the Hebrews had reclaimed the land of Canaan just as Yahweh had promised, Salmon and I settled down just outside the Jebusite city of Jerusalem. The fertile land produced wheat and barley so abundant that we baked the excess grain into bread to sell to our Jebusite neighbors. In time, our small village became known as the "House of Bread" or "Beth-le-hem."

Salmon and I lived in Bethlehem all the rest of our days. Our youngest son Boaz and his wife, Ruth, now live in our family home. And Yahweh has given me the assurance that my Boaz and Ruth (a foreign, former pagan Moabite) will become the ancestors of our great King David and through David will come the Messiah — Jesus the Christ!

Don't ever forget. Our God is a God of new beginnings. Remember how my life was, a heathen and a prostitute. Yet, God understood all my confusion. All I had to offer him was brokenness and strife, but he made something beautiful of my life. He is ready, willing and able to do the same for you.

Thank you for allowing me to share my story with you.

RUTH

Character: *Ruth*

Caption: *The Great-Grandmother Of King David*

Publicity Blurb: *"Do you know what it is like to be widowed at the age of twenty, and move to a foreign country with only your mother-in-law for companionship?"*

Scripture: *Ruth 4:13-17*

Hymns: *"He Leadeth me, O Blessed Thought;" "Great Is Thy Faithfulness"; "The Gift Of Love"*

Scripture Study Prep: *The Book of Ruth*

Length of Performance: *word count 3,147*

Dress: *brown robe with head drape*

Shoes: *biblical sandals*

Accessories: *wooden or beaded accessories*

Props: *sheaf of dried wheat, homemade scroll with scripture from Ruth 2:16,17*

Make-up: *usual*

Suggested Season to Perform: *Valentine's Day with its emphasis on love*

Explanations: *Might mention that Oprah Winfry's mother accidentally misspelled her daughter's name. She meant to name her "Orpah." Also, the field where the shepherds were keeping watch that first Christmas night was in Boaz's field, still pointed out to tourists in Israel today.*

Ruth

A young, foreign, pagan widow (Great-Grandmother Of King David)

Hello. My name is Ruth, a name which translates as "friend" or "companion", and I hope I have lived up to that name. I grew up in the land of Moab which lies along the southeast shore of the Salt Sea. Moab is now a part of the present country of Jordan. My parents were religious people, worshiping the god Chemosh.

As I was approaching womanhood, a family from the land of Judah moved into our neighborhood, escaping a severe drought in their country. They seemed nice enough, but because they worshiped the Israelite God Yahweh, my parents forbade me to associate with them. I didn't understand why. I would have given the matter no further thought, except that within the family were two handsome sons of marrying age. Their names were Mahlon and Chillion. My best friend, Orpah (not Oprah), and I decided to check the boys out. Before long, a four-way friendship had developed, much to the dismay of all our parents.

But you know how teenagers are. The more our parents tried to pull us apart, the more we felt drawn together. Then after a sudden illness, Mahlon's father, Elimelech, died. I was afraid that, as eldest son and now head of the family, Mahlon might reject me in favor of a woman from his own country. But that did not happen.

As soon as the mourning period was over, he announced his plans to take me as his bride. Chilion followed suit, announcing his intentions toward Orpah. Against strong protest from their mother, Naomi, whose name means "pleasant", we were married and both Orpah and I went to live on the farm of Elimelech.

Though my mother-in-law had violently opposed our union, as soon as the marriage was official, she accepted me with open arms. Orpah and I worked side-by-side with our husbands, building the small farm into a successful enterprise.

Several years went by. Life was good, but Naomi seemed obsessed that neither Orpah nor I had borne children. I was not upset. I wanted children, but we were young. We had plenty of time.

Then, suddenly, our world was turned upside down. An epidemic swept through our land and in only two weeks both Mahlon and Chilion lay dead.

As Orpah and I grieved the loss of our husbands, Naomi bore the grief of the loss of both her sons, and the added grief of the fact that no issue had been born to Mahlon or Chilion. Her beloved Elimelech's line would end. Never in the sacred genealogy of her people would the descendants of Elimelech be read aloud.

One day a traveler from Judah stopped at our home for rest and refreshment. As was the custom in Judah, we received him graciously, cared for his needs, and washed his feet. He repaid our hospitality with news from Judah. The famine was over. Harvests were bountiful once more.

A week later Naomi told us the news. She had decided to go home. She had been worried about her husband's farm back in Judah since her sons' death. A woman could not ordinarily hold property, and now that her sons were gone, their property was in danger of being taken away. But *if* she was there, perhaps she could figure out a way to save the farm. Orpah and I both agreed immediately to return with her, but Naomi felt that we would be better off to remain in our own country near our relatives. She explained that, because we were both young and beautiful, but more importantly because we had not borne children, our parents would be able to find us husbands.

"But, how will you survive?" I asked.

She told me that Moses had given instructions to her people to "care for" the widows and orphans, and she was now a widow. We still wanted to go with her; after all we were widows, too. But she feared for our well-being. You see, not only were we widowed, we were also foreign and heathens.

On the day Naomi was to leave, I showed up just as Orpah and Naomi were saying goodbye. My little cart was loaded with all I owned that I could reasonably carry with me. I told my mother-in-law that I had made up my mind and that my place was with her. Again, she tried to dissuade me from going. I spoke to her from my heart, saying words that I understand you use today in your marriage vows. Here, I wrote it down so I could say it correctly. (hold up scroll)

"Mother Naomi", I said, *"entreat me not to leave thee, or to return from following after thee; for whether thou goest, I will go: and where thou lodgeth, I will lodge; thy people shall be my people, and thy God my God: where thou diest, will I die, and there will I be buried; the Lord do so to me, and more also, if aught but death part thee and me."*[8]

Tears streamed down Naomi's face, and my face, and Orpah's. We embraced, then Naomi and I turned and began our journey; she to her familiar home, I to a strange land.

In the desert of Moab, the April days were already long and hot. We moved slowly, traveling only in the cool of each morning. A lean-to tent provided shelter from the midday sun. By nightfall the wind arose and a chill settled over the land.

In the long afternoons as we lay in the shade, I asked Naomi to tell me again the stories of her people and her God, Yahweh. I had heard the stories ever since I had married into the family. But now that Yahweh was *my* God, and Israelite people *my* people, the stories took on added importance.

She told of the creation and the flood, of Abraham as he settled the promised land. Many of the stories had always been well known to me. After all, the Moabite people were descendants of Abraham's nephew Lot. Other stories, such as the mighty exodus out of Egypt and the military exploits of Joshua, were less well-known. My favorite story was the one about Rahab, the harlot, who lived in Jericho and had hidden the spies of Israel and as a result, had been saved when Jericho fell to the Hebrew people.

"What happened to Rahab after that?" I asked Naomi.

"She married an Israelite", Naomi had answered. She continued her story. "Joshua gave her to one of the soldiers, Salmon, and after the fighting to recapture the promised land, they settled south of the Jebusite city of Jerusalem. The land was very fertile and the climate so agreeable that they were able to grow and harvest three plantings of grain a season. They planted

8 Ruth 1:16,17 (NRSV).

emmer wheat, barley and rye. So plentiful were their crops, that they sold baked bread to the residents of Jerusalem. As Salmon's family and compound grew, the settlement became known as *Beth* (house) *le* (of) *hem* (bread) — Beth-le-hem, 'the house of bread.' Actually, Bethlehem is not far from our farm. I think their youngest son, Boaz, still lives in their family home." Then, I could see the light go on the Naomi's eyes. Boaz, she had just remembered, was a cousin of Elimelech, and wealthy, too.

For the rest of the journey, Naomi planned and schemed, trying out first one scenario and then another. Apparently, Israel still retained a little-used law called the Levirate marriage law. On the death of a man, his brother or next of kin, was obligated to marry the widow. The first child of that union would inherit the dead man's property. This law was to ensure that the property would stay in the family since a woman could not hold title to the land. Naomi had decided that I would marry Boaz and my first child would then inherit Elimelech's property.

Naomi was very proud of herself. She had just solved all our problems. I was not so sure. It seemed to me that Boaz would have a say about the plan. What if he was married? Could he have two wives? But Naomi was not worried. "This is the will of Yahweh," she would say. "I'm sure of it. God will take care of me. God will take care of us."

When we arrived in Bethlehem, we had hardly unpacked before Naomi was out tracking down Boaz, finding out all the latest gossip, where he would be at a certain time. She was not leaving anything to chance.

As it turned out, a nearby barley field, ready for harvest, was owned by Boaz, who just happened to be a widower. This was perfect for her plan. We needed food badly and the law of Moses required farmers to leave some grain behind for the poor who were willing to go out and work in the fields. Naomi announced that, come daybreak, I would be in Boaz's field gleaning barley. I would be sure to meet him that way. I obeyed.

I rose long before day and was waiting in the field when the workers arrived. All morning I worked. My back and hands felt as though they had been trampled by the oxen in the field. As noon-time approached, I noticed Boaz's arrival. His garment signified him as a landowner, a man of great wealth. Turquoise jewels embedded in the bridle of the black Arabian stallion glistened in the sun. I paused from my work to get a good look at this kinsman of my late husband.

He did not in any way resemble the picture I had painted in my mind. He was a very small man, seeming shorter than he actually was because his shoulders were slightly slumped. His hair was reddish brown. His skin, though darkened by the sun, still had the look of a light-skinned, red-haired person. And, unlike a fine wine, his 58 years had not aged him well. In all, he was not what any young, beautiful woman would find attractive.

But I have always been a practical woman, and this man could be my salvation. Over and over I said to myself, "This is the man Naomi has picked for me. I must be kind to him for Naomi's sake, for my sake. He can be our deliverer. He can be our protector. I must be gracious to him. After all, physical appearance is not really important."

When lunch time came, Boaz's foreman approached me. I was afraid he would tell me that I had gleaned enough from this field and would have to move on down the road. Instead, he offered me an invitation to join Boaz and the workers for lunch. My heart raced within me. Naomi's plan was working.

Boaz greeted me, introduced himself, and stated that we were practically kin, since I was the widow of his cousin. As he talked, I noticed his eyes. In that moment, I knew that Naomi and Yahweh were right. This was the man for me.

Each day Boaz would find some excuse to stop by and talk. We shared our noon meal together. Each evening I would tell Naomi everything he had said or done.

When the harvesting was completed, I was sad but Naomi was ecstatic. "Now I can put the final part of my plan into action," she announced.

This was the plan. The threshing took place in a large barn built over the large flat rock Abraham had used as an altar when he thought he was going to have to sacrifice his son Isaac.[9]

9 The Dome of the Rock in Jerusalem is built on this rock

The work of threshing was difficult. But when the harvest was plentiful, as it had been this year, the threshing took on a festive air with beer flowing freely. The work would take several days. The women went home each night but the men camped out on the floor of the barn. They worked hard, drank freely, and then slept soundly.

I was to hide in the barn until all the men were asleep, then slip quietly to where Boaz lay. I was to lift his covers and lie down at his feet. In this way I would be asking, not only that he spread his blanket over me to protect me from the night air, but symbolically, to spread his blanket of protection over me, to take me as his wife. If Boaz reacted favorably, if he embraced me, made love to me, then he was agreeing to become my "go-el" - my legal protector.

It all sounded strange to me. That was not the way we did things in Moab. But I was no longer in Moab. If this was the way it was done in Israel, then this was the way I would do it.

Naomi scrubbed me until I lost at least two layers of skin. She poured scented oil over me, dressed me in the finest clothes and jewelry we owned, and sent me on my way. When I reached the barn, I sneaked into the threshing hall and secretly watched until Boaz lay down to sleep. When I was certain that all of the men were asleep, I slipped over to Boaz, lifted his covers and lay down at his feet.

During the night Boaz awoke startled. "Who are you? And what are you doing down at my feet?" he asked roughly.

"I am Ruth," I responded meekly. "Spread your covering over your maidservant for you are next of kin." I had learned my lines well.

Boaz seemed pleased. "Ruth, I didn't recognize you in the dark. But what on earth are you doing lying down there at my feet?"

"I'm only following Naomi's instructions," I said. "She told me to wait until you were asleep, then to lift your covers and lie down at your feet. And that is what I have done."

"Oh, foolish girl," laughed Boaz. "You have much to learn about the subtleties of our language."

"What do you mean?" I asked, almost not wanting the answer because it was obvious that I had done something dumb.

"'*Feet*' is just a polite way of saying a word that she was too embarrassed to say," he said, enjoying my discomfort. "I assure you that down there at my feet is not where Naomi had in mind for you to lie. Come on up here, girl, where you belong. Now, tell me again what you were saying."

And, so, I repeated the words I had memorized, "I am Ruth. Spread your covering over your maidservant for you are next of kin."

"I think I understand the situation," he said softly. "You are evoking the old Levirate marriage law. You are willing to sacrifice yourself to a rich, old ugly man for Naomi's sake. This kindness is greater than any you have done previously for her."

I admitted that that had been my motivation in the beginning, but that my feelings for him had changed. I summoned my courage and asked him again to take me as his wife. He assured me that he was more than willing to make me his bride, *if* I was sure that that was what I really wanted.

Once he had spoken those words of acceptance to me a calmness settled over us and all awkwardness vanished. Cuddled in his arms, we talked quietly. I could not see his face, his eyes, but I could see his form silhouetted against the moonlight. His voice was deep and warm. His arms were strong and tender. A man had not held me in his arms for a very long time.

The protection of a man felt good again. I was so tired of being strong. My strength had protected me through my husband's death, through the trip into the foreign land, through caring for a sweet, but sometimes cantankerous, mother-in-law. Now, there would be someone to care for me.

He embraced me tightly. I responded to his every touch, readily melting into his arms. He kissed me, first tenderly, then passionately. Then, suddenly, he pulled away.

"Oh, no!" I thought. "I have made a fool of myself again. He was only playing with me. I've got to get out of here!" I began to scramble out of the covers, but he grabbed me and pulled me close to him. "Let me go!" I said, loudly enough to wake the other men. "You don't want me, you were only teasing me."

"No, no, you've got it all wrong," he said. "I want you very much. I want you as my wife. But we've got a problem. I am not Mahlon and Elimelech's closest relative. Manoah has first claim on you."

"Do you think he will want to marry me?" I asked.

"I'm afraid so. He's had his eye on Elimelech's property for a long time."

We lay together and talked of things that might have been. Finally, we slept. Just before daybreak Boaz awakened me, so that I could slip out of the threshing barn unseen.

"Don't worry", he said as we parted, "I'll find a way somehow." I believed him. And when I told Naomi of the problem, she was not upset. "Yahweh will find a way," she responded.

To make a long story short, my Boaz did find a way for us to be legally married. It had something to do with throwing a sandal at somebody. But we *were* married. I went to live with him in his family home there in Bethlehem, the home Salmon had built for Rahab, the heathen. Like her, I had found a home with a new God and a loving husband.

The following year, I gave birth to a son. Naomi was delirious with joy. Elimelech's line had not ended. In little Obed lay the accumulation of generations of believers, of Abraham, Isaac, and Jacob. As I looked into his face, (after first counting his fingers and toes), I dreamed the dream of all mothers. Someday my son, Obed, would be famous in the land of Judah and in the land of Israel. And, if not Obed, then his son Jesse, or *his* son David.

I silently praised Yahweh for his graciousness. From a barren widow in a foreign land to a wealthy wife and mother; from a pagan who worshiped an idol to a true believer of Yahweh. God is so good.

And I've also come to realize a great truth. God could not have restored my life, brought me happiness, contentment, and joy *if* I had not been willing to take a chance, to leave my home and relatives and venture into a strange land trusting in the one and only God, Yahweh.

Dear friends, don't be afraid if Yahweh is calling you to something just as unknown, unfamiliar. Trust him. He will never let you down.

MARY

Character: *Mary*

Caption: *The One And Only Virgin Mother*

Publicity Blurb: *"Can you imagine being thirteen years old and trying to explain your miraculous conception to your parents and of giving birth to the Holy Child in a stable stall?"*

Scripture: *Luke 1:30,31; 2:7*

Hymns: *"Come, Thou Long-Awaited Jesus"*

Scripture Study Prep: *Luke, Chapters 1-2*

Length of Performance: *word count 3,475*

Dress: *blue robe, light blue head drape*

Shoes: *biblical sandals*

Accessories: *star of David necklace*

Props: *none*

Make-up: *usual*

Suggested Season to Perform: *Advent*

Mary

The One And Only Virgin Mother

Hello. Thank you for inviting me here during this season of Advent — your season of waiting and preparing to celebrate the remembrance of the great event. I want to share with you my story of that most holy night so long ago. I'm sure you all know the story well, but I'd like for you to hear it from me as I remember it.

But, before I tell my story, let me give you a little of the history of my people. I come from a people who waited for the Messiah for hundreds of years. The first prophecy of the long-awaited Messiah was in the Garden of Eden. Did you know that? When God is dealing with the sin of Adam and Eve and of the serpent, he tells the serpent that one day, one of Eve's descendants will be born that will crush that serpent's head.

So, from the very beginning, we had been waiting and watching for the Messiah. My ancestor Abraham was promised land, land, and more land — that all-important promised land; and promised descendants numerous as the stars or the grains of sand. But, then through a series of events, from Abraham, then Isaac, then Jacob, my people ended up in Egypt in slavery. We were there four hundred years. And, in all those four hundred years, our people prayed for a Messiah, for a deliverer, for the one who would come and lead our people out of slavery.

And, then, he came. It wasn't our long-awaited Messiah, but it was a great leader. It was Moses. And he did lead our people out of Egypt. But he, himself, didn't make it to the promised land. His successor, Joshua, (Ye-shu-a), was the one who actually led our people back into that promised land. How fitting that his name was "Joshua", for that name means "God is salvation." And, under his leadership, God was our salvation, our deliverer.

But we found out that there were still enemies in the land. There were the Canaanites and other tribes. By the time I was born, the Roman government occupied my country. And, again we longed for a Messiah. We searched and studied the scriptures.

There, in the scriptures, we found references to his birth in Bethlehem of Judea, even one passage stated that "Out of Egypt shall I call my son." We read the words from Isaiah, "For unto you (a virgin) a child shall be born, a child whose name shall be called Wonderful Counselor, Mighty God, Everlasting Father, Prince of Peace." It was all very confusing. Our Messiah from Egypt? Born of a virgin? But we waited, we watched, and we prayed.

Now, let me tell you my personal story. I tell you I know something about waiting, not waiting to celebrate the remembrance of the long-awaited Messiah but waiting for the actual birth of the Messiah. Have you ever thought about the fact that I, personally, waited nine months for the birth of the Christ child?

I was born and raised in the city of Nazareth, about seventy miles north of Jerusalem. My parents were God-fearing people and we attended sabbath services each week at the synagogue. Of course, Mother and I had to stay in the curtained off section because we were "only women". My brothers attended school at the synagogue. Oh, how I wished I could have gone to school, but it was considered useless to formally educate a woman. After all, a woman's place was in the home. But Mother did home school me.

I was an obedient child. And as I grew up, I was still obedient. But like most teenagers, I was somewhat irresponsible and sometimes clumsy. When I was twelve years old, I began my menses, which marked my introduction into womanhood. Shortly afterward, I was betrothed to an older man in town by the name of Joseph. He was a godly man, greatly revered in the community. It was said that he was a "dreamer of dreams"; that God communicated to him through dreams and visions. I wasn't exactly enthusiastic about the match, but I knew he would be good to me. We went through the formal betrothal ceremony, pledging me to him in marriage. It was like a great big engagement celebration. Then Joseph gave me back to my father to live at home for a full year, until I had matured a little. Though the marriage would not be sexually consummated for a year, I was legally considered his wife.

I spent that year preparing to be a wife, learning to run a household. I took over much of my mother's duties of cooking and cleaning, sewing and caring for the younger children. One of my favorite activities was teaching my younger sisters, who could not attend synagogue school since they were girls, teaching them and a few of their little friends some of the great stories my mother had taught me from the Bible. You all know the ones I mean: Adam and Eve and the beautiful garden, Noah and the great flood, Joseph and his coat of many colors, Moses at the Red Sea, and King David when he was only a teenager, fighting the giant Goliath.

And then one day, the most remarkable thing happened. Late one afternoon, I was sitting alone in the house sewing, and an angel appeared. I don't know if the angel was really there, or if it was a vision. All I know is that I wasn't dreaming. I was scared. The angel was beautiful, but I was still scared. Then he called me by name, "Mary," he said, "Don't be afraid. You have found favor with God. Behold you shall conceive and bring forth a son. And you shall call his name 'Jesus'." There's that name again. "Jesus" is a variation of the name "Joshua", "God is salvation." Remember?

I can't believe I had the chutzpah to argue with an angel, but I did. "How can this be?" I asked. "I have never slept with a man."

"The Holy Ghost shall come upon you, and the power of the highest shall overshadow you, and that holy thing which shall be born of you shall be called the Son of God."

The angel went on to say something about my cousin Elizabeth who was also miraculously with child, but I was still trying to take in the fact that I was to give birth to the Son of God. All I could do was murmur, "Behold, the handmaiden of the Lord. Be it unto me according to thy word."

Then the angel left and I fell into a sleep. When my mother came home, she found me lying in the floor and was afraid I was sick. She was bewildered when I mumbled something about giving birth to the Son of God. She wrapped me up in a quilt and brought me some hot tea to drink. "Now, tell me what happened," she said, "speak slowly and start at the beginning."

This I did. I told her everything that happened. "Sweetheart," she said comfortingly, "you just had a dream. I imagine it's all your anxiety about becoming a wife. Don't worry. Joseph is a good man. He will be gentle with you."

I decided Mother was probably right. It had all been a dream. But it seemed so real. A few weeks later, I missed my monthly time of blood. At first, I wasn't too worried, because I wasn't extremely regular. But, as the days passed, the words of the angel came back to me over and over. I was to have a child by the Holy Ghost. But that just couldn't happen. I knew the miracles in the holy scriptures. But miracles don't happen in the lives of everyday people, especially a twelve year old and never a miracle like having a baby when you haven't had sex with a man.

Then, I began to experience subtle changes in my body. And although I had never been pregnant before, I had a "knowing" deep inside that I was pregnant now. I didn't know what to do. So I did what girls always do. I told my mother. She still didn't believe me about my angel encounter, but she did believe that I was pregnant. She was a practical woman, and she loved me very much. She immediately began to devise a strategy. I could visit my cousin Elizabeth who lived in the hill country.

"Oh, wonderful!" I exclaimed, "She is with child, too."

"Where on earth did you get an idea like that?" Mother asked. "Elizabeth is barren. You know that."

"Not anymore," I replied.

Father wondered about my sudden trip but did not interfere with our plans. I was eager to see Elizabeth, to see for myself that she was pregnant. When I arrived at her home I rushed in, calling her name. She greeted me excitedly and said, "Oh, Mary, when you called out, I felt the baby within me leap for the first time! Oh, who am I that the mother of my Lord should come to me?"

Then she said the most beautiful thing. "Mary, Blessed art thou among women, and blessed is the fruit of thy womb."

My heart overflowed and a song of praise welled up inside me. "My soul doth magnify the Lord, and my spirit hath rejoiced in God my Savior, for he hath regarded the low estate of his handmaiden; for behold, from henceforth all generations shall call me blessed."

My song of praise went on and on, with Elizabeth joining in from time to time. When the singing and praising was over, Elizabeth and I hugged and cried. Then, we settled down to catch up on family gossip. Elizabeth told me of her husband's remarkable encounter. Zacharias, who was a priest, was offering incense before the Lord when the angel Gabriel appeared to him. The angel announced to him the miraculous birth of their son whom they were to name John. And when Zacharias expressed disbelief to the angel (for Elizabeth had been barren for many, many years) the angel struck him dumb. The angel told him he would not be able to speak again until the birth of their child. When I heard that, I trembled slightly. I had back-talked that same angel also. How fortunate that I was not struck dumb or worse.

I stayed with them for several weeks. Each day Elizabeth and I would study with Zacharias. Though he could not speak, he pointed out all the prophecies in our scriptures of the coming of the Messiah. And each day my faith grew stronger. Finally, I was ready to go home and face my fate, whatever it might be.

When I returned home, Mother was glad to see me, but fearful for my safety when I insisted on telling Father everything. My father loved me as much as Mother did. But he was also a rigid man who believed in following the letter of the law. Not only did he not believe my story about the angel, he considered my claim to be outright blasphemous. He also felt that telling Joseph was the only honorable thing to do.

With a heavy heart, he made his way to Joseph's house to confess my "sin" and plead for mercy. You see, a pregnancy by a man other than my betrothed was not viewed as a youthful indiscretion which could be forgiven. Because of my betrothal, I was now legally Joseph's wife and therefore, not guilty of fornication, but adultery! And the most severe punishment for adultery was death by stoning. The only way a sentence could be commuted was if the injured man, Joseph in my case, would agree to having me banished instead.

When my father related my circumstance to Joseph, he was first outraged, his pride wounded. But because he was a just and compassionate man, he offered to "put me away quietly" that is, not to have me stoned or to banished me, but allow me to go away somewhere else to live — at least until the baby came. Then, I could return to the village, but I would live in shame because of my indiscretion. I slept little that night. I was only thirteen years old. I didn't understand what was happening or why. I knew I had done no wrong. The angel said I had found favor with God. But my life certainly didn't look like God was favoring me.

Imagine our surprise the next morning when Joseph came to our house and offered to honor the betrothal. "But why would you offer to do this?" asked my incredulous father. "Because," Joseph answered, "an angel appeared to me last night in a dream. And he said unto me, 'Do not fear to take Mary as your wife, for that which is conceived in her is of the Holy Ghost. And she shall bring forth a son, and you shall call his name 'Jesus'; for he shall save his people from their sins.'"

My life had been spared! Joseph believed me! I was not in this exciting, but frightening, adventure alone. We could not go ahead and marry, however, because the law required that one must be betrothed for a full year before the formal wedding ceremony. (You know how important tradition is!) So I continued to live at my father's home, seeing Joseph only in the presence of a chaperone. I angered the townspeople by continuing to wear my blue head wrap. You see, only virgins wore pale blue. And as I grew bigger and bigger, obviously pregnant, they were outraged that I still pretended to be a virgin. But I knew I was a virgin, and Joseph agreed to let me continue to wear the blue.

A couple of weeks before the baby was due, a decree was issued demanding a census so that Rome could be sure they were getting the full tribute owed to them. Because Joseph was legally a resident of Bethlehem, (of the house and lineage of David) he was required to journey to Bethlehem to register and he felt I should accompany him. My mother told him, in no uncertain terms, that I was in no condition to make that trip. But Joseph was unmoved. Even my father appealed to Joseph. "Contact the authorities," he said, "they will make an exception in your case, I'm sure." But again Joseph was unmoved. I didn't understand Joseph's actions.

He had always seemed so concerned for my well-being. He knew how hard the trip would be on me. But Joseph was my husband. If he said that I must go, then I must go.

As we prepared for the journey, Joseph said quietly, "Mary, do not fear, for this journey is God's will." "How do you know?" I asked. "Have you had another vision? Did an angel appear to you?" "No," he said, "but the day before the decree came, I was studying the holy scriptures once again. I was reading in the book of Micah these words: "But thou, Bethlehem Ephratah, though thou be little among the thousands of Judah, yet out of thee shall come forth unto me that which is to be ruler in Israel". I wondered how your son could be born in Bethlehem. And then the decree came. See, it is God's will."

Oh, I won't pretend that I understood hardly anything that was happening. But I did trust. I trusted in God, and I trusted in my husband. I started out on the journey in good spirits. But seventy miles on a donkey in your ninth month will sour anyone's spirits. I thought my back would break in two. There were many bathroom breaks, and several nights on the road, sleeping on the ground. But through it all, Joseph kept quoting scripture and comforting me. "Just hold on until we reach Bethlehem, then everything will be all right."

And I did. I held to the vision of giving birth to the Son of God in a beautiful home, with kings bowing before us. But when we got to Bethlehem, (which is just a few miles south of Jerusalem), it was late — well past bedtime, and there was absolutely no room for us anywhere. Joseph had friends and relatives in Bethlehem, but they were all the way on the other side of the city and it was too late to seek them out. And, I knew we didn't have the time to make it to the other side of the city. I hadn't told Joseph, but the labor pains had started several hours earlier. Finally, at one somewhat disreputable-looking inn, the wife of the innkeeper took pity on me.

"Honey," she said to her husband, "they could use the stable, couldn't they?" "They wouldn't want a stable," he gruffly replied. "A stable would be good!" we both cried aloud together. "Where is it?" Joseph asked. "Out back, where do you think?" the man replied. Joseph thanked him and we quickly made our way to the stable. The stable turned out, not to be a freestanding structure, but a small cave. Well, not really a cave, just an overhanging ledge which went about thirty or forty feet back into the hillside. It was dirty, smelly, and full of animals. But it was also dry and out of the wind. And I couldn't bear another minute on that donkey.

We hadn't been in the cave more than thirty minutes when the labor pains started in earnest. I panicked. Not only was my mother not here, but there was no midwife. No one to help me, except Joseph. But Joseph was wonderful. He spread out clean hay and covered it with the blanket from the donkey. He talked soothingly to me, again quoting all the Messianic promises from our holy scriptures. "I don't know why God has chosen this way to bring his son into the world," Joseph said, "but I do know that God has chosen this method. Do not fear, Mary, God is in control."

And so it was that on that holy night, in a stable in Bethlehem, I brought forth my firstborn son, (and after looking into the face of my precious child — literally the Son of God — and counting his fingers and toes) I wrapped him in swaddling clothes, and laid him in a manger.

Then, I laid back and took a long-deserved sleep. I don't know how long I slept, but I was awakened by Joseph who said that we had visitors. Well, you women might understand this. I was not in the mood for visitors. I was certainly not ready for the visitors as far as my appearance went. I looked like I had just spent seventy miles on the back of a donkey and given birth in a stable. I told Joseph to please send them away, but Joseph calmly assured me that these visitors had a story I wanted to hear.

It was a group of shepherds who were out keeping their watch over their flock by night, when suddenly an angel — a very large angel — appeared in the sky and the glory of the Lord shone round about them, and they were sore afraid. The angel told them "Fear not; for behold, I bring you good tidings of great joy, which shall be to all people. For unto you is born this day in the city of David, a Savior which is Christ the Lord. And this shall be a sign unto you: you shall find the babe wrapped in swaddling clothes and laying in a manger." Then, suddenly with that angel was a multitude of the heavenly host, praising God and saying: "Glory to God in the highest, and on earth — peace, goodwill toward men." Then the angels went away and the sky was dark again.

They said that when the angels had gone away, they said to one another, "Let us now go and see this thing which the Lord has made known unto us." And they came with haste to find us.

They visited with us briefly, kneeling before that feed trough and offering their prayers. Then, as they left they did a very strange thing. Rather than turning their backs and simply walking out of the stable, they backed out of the stable as one does when leaving the presence of a king.

Then, they were gone and I was left with only Joseph and my Holy Child. But I kept all these things that I've told you and pondered them in my heart.

Again, I want to thank you for allowing me to come and retell the old, old story with you of that holy night so long ago.

Thank you.

MARY

Character: *Mary*

Caption: *The Grieving Mother Of Our Lord*

Publicity Blurb: *"Can you imagine the horror and disbelief as I held the dead body of my miraculous son, the son who came to earth to defeat death?"*

Scripture: *John 19: 25-27*

Hymns: *"Were You There?"*

Scripture Study Prep: *Luke, Chapter 23*

Length of Performance: *word count 3,117*

Dress: *blue robe with dark blue or black head wrap*

Shoes: *biblical sandals*

Accessories: *star of David necklace*

Props: *statuette of the "Pieta" on square cloth of purple*

Make-up: *usual*

Suggested Season to Perform: *Lent, especially Holy Week*

Mary

The Grieving Mother Of Our Lord

Hello, my name is Mary. The name "Mary" or "Miriam" means "strong". And somehow my parents chose that name well, for I have had to be strong. I'm sure you know my story well; how the power of the almighty came upon me and I conceived and bore Jesus, the Messiah. After my husband's disturbing vision, Joseph, the baby and I fled to Egypt just hours before the soldiers of Herod killed all the boy babies in Bethlehem under two years of age. We lived in Egypt until we received word that Herod had died and that it was safe to return home.

Back in my hometown of Nazareth, our lives settled down into a comfortable routine. All the gossip that had surrounded my first pregnancy had died down and we led a normal life. Jesus was an astute student of the holy scriptures which were taught at the synagogue school. He was courteous and kind, fun to be around. Everybody loved him. I guess you could say *he grew in wisdom and in stature and in favor with God and man.*[10]

One event happened when he was twelve years old that caused me to ponder again the miraculous nature of his birth. We, along with many from our town, had made the pilgrimage to Jerusalem for Passover. The week was exciting, as always, but nothing unusual occurred. On the day of departure, we set out on the return journey, the adults leading the way with the older children tagging along behind.

At nightfall, when supper was prepared, I called the children. They all came quickly, hungry after a day on the road. But Jesus was not with them. I searched but could not find him. I was not overly concerned, for Jesus never gave me any trouble. When his father returned to our campsite, I sent him out to find Jesus. Joseph searched every campsite. Jesus was nowhere to be found. The fear of every parent had come true. We had gone on a trip and accidentally left our child behind.

10 Luke 2:52 (NIV)

I wanted to start out immediately, but my husband explained that the roads were much too dangerous to travel at night, so we had to wait until morning to retrace our steps. I didn't sleep a wink that night. At first light, we were on our way. I prayed every mile of the journey. Once in Jerusalem it took us three days to find Jesus. We found him, of all places, in the temple arguing scripture with the learned doctors of theology. Any of you who are mothers know my reaction. I was, at once, both greatly relieved to find my son well and safe, and greatly agitated that he had caused us so much grief.

"Son!" I exclaimed, "Why have you done this to us? We were sick with worry."

I will never forget my son's answer or the authority in his voice. He looked me in the face, not in haughtiness, but with detachment and asked, *"How is it that you sought me? Do you not understand that I must be about my Father's business?"*[11]

No, I didn't understand what he meant. But I kept that reply in my mind along with the events surrounding his conception and his birth. And over the years, I pondered all these things in my heart. Well, the years passed. Jesus and his brothers and sisters grew into adulthood. Jesus studied for a while at the Essene community at Qumran, but returned home to take over the carpentry shop when my husband died and to assume his role as "head of the family".

For many years, Jesus seemed content working with wood, studying the scriptures, and sharing his faith with a few close friends. Some even called him "Rabbi", though he was never officially appointed by the synagogue.

Then one day, Jesus went down to the River Jordan near Bethabara to hear his cousin John preach. John was baptizing the listeners who had repented of their sins. I was not there that day. (I never cared much for John's fiery style of preaching). But I am told that Jesus approached his cousin requesting to be baptized. At first, John refused, saying that it was he who should be baptized of Jesus. I would have made that trip just to hear John say something humbling.

11 Luke 2:49 (RGT)

But Jesus insisted that John baptize him. Walking waist deep in the river, John scooped up water in an empty ram's horn and poured it over Jesus' head. Some, who were there that day, said that immediately the heavens opened up, and they heard a voice from heaven saying, *"This is my beloved Son, in whom I am well pleased."* Others said that they "sensed" something (a spirit, maybe) which seemed to descend upon Jesus almost like a dove. Still others said that they neither saw, heard nor sensed anything unusual.

After the baptism, Jesus sent word to me by a neighbor telling me that he was going away for a time of prayer and fasting. I assumed he was going into the barren mountains near Jericho where many holy men would seclude themselves from time to time for just such a time of prayer and fasting. I assumed he would be home within a few days. But that didn't happen. A week went by, then two weeks, then three weeks. In all, forty days went by without a word from my son.

Then one day, he appeared in my doorway. Again, like that time when he was twelve years old, I was both so happy and thankful that he was home safe and sound, and at the same time, frustrated that he had put me through so much worry. I rushed to him, to give him a piece of my mind, but as I neared him, I could see that he was a changed man. He had a new look about him, even in the way he stood. As I got nearer to him and could see his face, I could tell that he had been with God.

Several days later, his cousin John and his disciples were walking along the road and saw Jesus approaching. Pointing to Jesus, John said to his men, *"Behold, the Lamb of God which taketh away the sins of the world."* Immediately, two of John's disciples left him to follow Jesus. Soon, there were ten others in Jesus' new circle of disciples.

Jesus began attracting a small, but faithful, following of townspeople. Those mysterious events surrounding his birth, the angel's prophecy, all came back to me. My son was, indeed, the Savior of the world. But he was so gentle and unassuming. He would never achieve much notice the way he was going about his ministry. So, I decided to help him out, the way mothers do.

We were invited to a wedding in Cana. Initially, Jesus did not want to go, but I insisted now that he was 'head of the family'. During the reception, our host ran short on wine. Now, maybe that would not be a big deal in your day, but in mine it was a great social faux pas. I saw my opportunity. I explained the man's dilemma and asked my son to perform a miracle by turning water into wine. At first, Jesus refused, saying "No, Mother, I can't do that." But I assured him that he had powers he didn't yet realize. "No, Mother," he said. *"My time has not yet come."* But, finally, because he was an obedient son, he did as I had requested.

He instructed the servants to fill six thirty-gallon stone water jars with water from the well and to take a sample to the wine steward. They did as he requested. The steward rushed to the host, declaring, *"Every man serves the good wine first; and when men have drunk freely, then the poor wine; but you have kept the good wine until now."*

The wedding was not only saved, but it was a great success. The host was quick to give credit for the good wine to Jesus and the word of his miracle spread. More and more townspeople began to be attracted to his teachings and his miracles — even some members of the Sanhedrin.

But I was worried about Jesus. He spoke harshly of some of the powerful religious leaders. I tried to warn him, suggesting that he soften his rhetoric. But he would not be swayed, even though it was apparent that opposition to him was mounting. I began to fear for his safety.

When Jesus was teaching nearby, I took two of his brothers and we went to see him. It was time that I had a mother-son talk with him, to again explain the mounting danger that he was in. When we reached the area where he was, the teaching session had concluded and Jesus had entered a home. I went up to the house and started to enter. I was stopped by a large, burly fisherman whom I recognized as Peter. I attempted to push Peter aside as I entered, but he blocked me.

"Get out of the way, Peter. I'm here to see my son."

"He can't see you now," he replied and continued to block my way.

"Then, you go tell him that his mother and brothers are here to see him." With that, Peter closed the door in my face. Boy, was I going to tell Jesus on Peter when I saw him.

Peter returned, opened the door, and again I started in. Again, he blocked my way.

"I told you, he can't see you now."

"Did you tell him that his mother and brothers were here to see him?"

"Yes," he replied.

"And, what did he say?"

"He said, 'Who is my mother? Who is my brother? The one who does the will of my Father, that is my mother, my brother, my sister.'"

Well, with that rebuke I turned and left. "Be that way," I thought. "I was only trying to help. Do it your own way."

I didn't see him anymore for a while, though I continued to pray for his well-being. When the time of Passover arrived, I decided to go to Jerusalem and stay with my sister, to observe the week-long festival. There were activities planned for every day. On the first day of the festivities, we heard that there was a great commotion over near the Eastern Gate, some sort of parade. So, I went to check it out.

When I arrived, I could hardly believe my eyes. Oh, there was a parade all right. There set Jesus upon a donkey with men, women, and children waving palm branches, laying their clothing in the street before him, and shouting, "Hosanna! Blessed is he that cometh in the name of the Lord. Blessed is the king of Israel."

I was horrified! Didn't Jesus understand the danger a demonstration like this would put him in, not to mention the claim that he was the king of Israel? Sometimes, I was amazed at the wisdom he always exhibited in spiritual matters and the lack of conventional wisdom he so often displayed in practical matters. I pushed through the crowds, trying to reach him, to urge him to take a low profile. But the crowd kept pushing me back.

I didn't see my son anymore during the five days of the Passover celebration. Then, on Friday morning, I received word that he had been arrested. My greatest fear had finally become a reality. My sister and another friend and I rushed down to the Antonio Fortress where Jesus was being tried. We couldn't get close because of the great multitude.

Pilate, the governor, was up on the second floor portico asking the crowd which prisoner he should release. This was a silly custom Pilate had instituted in honor of our Passover to curry favor with us. It didn't work. But here was Pilate asking the crowd which man he should release — Barabbas the murderer, or Jesus, the King of the Jews.

The crowd was shouting, *"Barabbas! Barabbas! Release to us Barabbas!"* I shouted, "No! Release Jesus!" Pilate had the soldiers untie his hands and Barabbas jumped down and joined his friends in the crowd. Then Pilate asked the people what he should do with Jesus, and the angry mob shouted back, *"Crucify him! Crucify him!"* I screamed at the top of my lungs, "No! No! Save Jesus! Save Jesus!" But my voice was lost in the clamor.

Pilate spoke to the crowd and said, *"I have examined this man and I find no fault with him."* But Pilate ordered the soldiers to take Jesus away to be scourged. When they brought him back, he was stripped of his clothing except for his loincloth, his back ripped and bleeding, blood trickling down from his forehead, and much of his beard pulled out by its roots, his face so swollen by the beating, I could hardly recognize him as my son. My knees grew weak. I would have slumped to the pavement if my sister had not been there to hold me up.

Again, Pilate asked the crowd, *"Now, What should I do with this man?"* Again, the crowd cried, *"Crucify him!"* *"Would you want me to kill your King?"* Pilate asked. *"We have no king but Caesar! We have no king but Caesar!"* they shouted. Then, fearing for his own political career, Pilate yielded to the crowd's demand, called for a basin of water, washed his hands and said to the crowd, *"I am innocent of this man's blood."* Then he ordered Jesus to be crucified.

The soldiers tied a large crossbeam across my son's raw back and led him through the streets to the place outside the city wall where all crucifixions took place — to Golgotha — to the place of the skull. Again, I tried to reach my son, to let him know that his mother was by his side. But, again, the crowd pushed me back.

By the time I got to the foot of the cross, Mary Magdalene, Joanna, and another Mary were already there. Soon, John, my son's closest friend, not his cousin but that disciple whom Jesus loved, joined us. I looked around but didn't see any of Jesus' other close friends. Peter wasn't there. James, Andrew, Judas — none of them were present.

I have never felt more helpless in all my life. There, on that hideous cross, hung my son, nails piercing his hands and feet. And just to show their contempt, the Roman soldiers had even stripped him of his loincloth, knowing the special shame nakedness held for a Jew.

And yet, naked and in torture, my son prayed to God for forgiveness for those who had done this horrible thing to him. I tried to get his attention, to let him know that his mother was here by his side, but I could not. Then, our eyes met. In waning strength, he looked down and spoke to me in halting words, *"Woman, behold thy son,"* as he looked over at his friend John who was standing beside me. And while looking at John he said, *"Behold thy mother,"* and looked back at me. I held his gaze as long as I could. It was as though the only two things he had left on earth were me and his friend and he was giving us to each other.

He spoke a few more times, each time weaker than before. Then, after a while longer, Jesus cried out in a surprisingly loud voice , *"It is finished! Father, unto thy hands I commend my spirit."* Then, he bowed his head, gave up the ghost and died.

Because his death had come so quickly, only a few hours and crucifixion could sometimes last for days, and as sundown was near, to make sure that he was dead, a soldier jabbed his spear into my son's side. Blood and water flowed mingled down, falling to the ground. With that act, I also fell to the ground in profound grief and confusion.

As the centurions lowered him from the cross, two wealthy men, Joseph of Arimathea and Nicodemus, a Pharisee, a member of the Sanhedrin, approached and received the body, wrapping it loosely with some cloths that were lying about.

John lovingly took Jesus' body and laid him in my arms. There, sitting on the ground, with the dead body of my little boy in my arms, memories flooded my mind — the surprising announcement by the angel that I would bear the Son of God; the angels heralding his birth; wise men traveling from far-off countries to bring him gifts; the special times we had as he was growing up; the voice from heaven at his baptism; the signs and wonders during his brief ministry. All my memories confirmed that he was, *indeed* the Son of God, the long-awaited Messiah; and you can't *kill* God!

Yet, here Jesus was dead! There was nothing to do but bury my son; bury the only begotten Son of God. And that we did. John took his body from my arms and handed him over to Joseph and Nicodemus. They carried his body to Joseph's nearby formal gardens where Joseph was in the midst of converting a small cave into a family tomb. John and Mary Magdalene supported me as I stumbled along behind.

At the tomb, the men gently laid Jesus' body on an empty slab. The slab on the other side was only half-hewn out, the tomb was so new. Now, his beaten and bloodied dead body lay there awaiting preparation for burial.

But, the hour of sabbath was fast approaching and our religion did not allow us to be out past sundown on sabbath. We had no choice but to leave and return after sabbath to finish the burial ritual — to ceremoniously wash the body, to anoint the body with oil and special burial spices, and to wrap the body tightly in fresh linens.

Joseph rolled a large stone across the opening of the tomb to protect the body from wild animals and we left. Night fell on us as we journeyed home. Darkness fell on all the earth that night. The hope of the world lay dead in a borrowed tomb.

Oh, the grief I bore! Oh, my friends,
Were you there when they crucified my son?
Were you there when they nailed him to the tree?
Were you there when we laid him in the tomb?
Were you there? Were you there?
Oh, excuse me…. Excuse me… *(exit crying)*

YOUNG MIRIAM

Character: *Jochebed's daughter — Miriam*

Caption: *Mother's Little Helper*

Publicity Blurb: *"Can you imagine having to cast your infant baby brother adrift on the Nile River in an attempt to spare his life?"*

Scripture: *Exodus 2:1-4*

Hymns: *"Lift Every Voice And Sing;" "We'll Understand It Better By And By;" "Stand By Me;" "Trust And Obey"*

Scripture Study Prep: *Exodus, Chapter 1 – 2:10*

Length of Performance: *word count 3,592*

Dress: *rose robe with head drape*

Shoes: *biblical sandals*

Accessories: *Egyptian jewelry*

Props: *wicker 'props' basket; baby blanket*

Make-up: *heavy eye liner, green eye shadow*

Suggested Season to Perform: *Mother's Day; Mother-Daughter Banquet*

Young Miriam

Mother's Little Helper

Hello, my name is Miriam, which means strong. My parents knew I had to be strong, because I was born into slavery in Egypt. Our people were not always in Egypt. Six hundred years earlier, our patriarch Abraham, who was living in the City of Ur in Southern Iraq, migrated with his family, led by God into the promised land of Canaan.

During his grandson Jacob's time, two hundred years later, a great famine covered our land, forcing Jacob to send two of his sons to Egypt to purchase food. When they got there, they found that the prime minister in charge of dispensing the grain was none other than their brother Joseph whom they had beaten up and sold into slavery years earlier. (Now, there's a long story which I don't have time to go into.)

Joseph had risen to this position through a series of dreams he interpreted for the Pharaoh, accurately predicting the years of famine, thereby allowing the Pharaoh to prepare for the upcoming famine, not only for his own people but for the surrounding countries, provided they could pay. And so, after an awkward reconciliation, Jacob and all his family moved into Egypt and settled in the land of Goshen, just to the northwest of the city you call Cairo.

For generations our people were treated well, for Joseph had averted so great a tragedy for the people of Egypt. Our people were honest and our number grew tremendously. But, after a couple of centuries, times change. I believe as one of your recorders of history put it, "There arose a Pharaoh who knew not Joseph." What that is referring to is the fact that the Hyksocs, also a Semitic people who had been living Egypt when Joseph was promoted to prime minister and our people migrated into Egypt, the Hyksocs were no longer in power. They had been overturned and the Egyptians had regained the throne. And, though we were not Hyksocs, we were Semitic, and therefore distrusted. Prejudice grew against my people. We were not of the correct "ethnic" stock. We were discriminated against, subtly at first.

But, over the years the discrimination grew harsher and harsher. Finally, the pharaoh set cruel taskmasters over my people. But still our number grew. The pharaoh became more uneasy. Finally, he subjected my people to outright slavery. And still our number increased, clearly a sign that our God was with us. The hatred and fear of us grew stronger, until the pharaoh was afraid of us, not so much of a slave uprising, but he feared that if, or perhaps I should say "when" his country was attacked, the large number of us would take over.

Let me stop and tell you a little about my family.

I was seven years old when the event I am about to relate to you occurred. I lived in the land of Goshen with my father Amram, my mother Jochebed (Yo-heav-id), which means "Jehovah is Glory", and my younger brother, Aaron. Life was certainly unpleasant being slaves, but we had a little bit of an advantage over the others. My parents were from the tribe of Levi, the priestly tribehood. My father was the current religious leader and was appointed a little more leniency than many of the other slaves. But I have to admit that my father was not much of a believer any longer.

You see, since this slavery had begun, and our people realized that we were trapped here, we had been praying for a deliverer, for a Savior. And as a religious leader, it was my father's duty to keep those prayers offered, to keep that hope alive. But even as a child of seven, I could see that my father's heart just wasn't in it. He and my mother had a number of discussions, down-right arguments about it. See, my mother's father had been the leading priest before my father. And she was so strong in her faith, she believed, truly, that God had not forgotten his people, but would send the deliverer.

And then, this awful decree! Pharaoh had ordered the midwives to kill all the newborn boy babies, letting only the girl babies live. If no midwife was present, then the father would have to throw the infant boy into the Nile River. Failure to do this would bring terrible punishment upon his entire family. And Mother had just realized that she was pregnant! I felt so helpless. I loved my mother so much. But, what could we do? Pray for daughter. Pray that the new baby would be a little girl. Mother took care to let no one know that she was pregnant. I prayed really hard for a baby sister. Mother kept saying, "God will deliver my baby, just as God will one day deliver my people."

When her time came, we made certain that it was in secret, in case it was a boy. And sure enough, it was a boy. A big, bouncy, beautiful baby boy. Oh, the horror of it all! We could not, we would not throw our baby into the river. But we knew that when he was discovered, a soldier would drown that precious child. We kept him hidden as best we could. But have you ever tried to keep an infant hidden and quiet? Oh, it was so difficult.

Then, one day Father came in and told us that our secret was out. One of the men he worked with had told a friend that he suspected that we were harboring a child and he was going the next day to report his suspicion to Pharaoh's men in hopes of a reward. Our luck had run out. Yet, strangely, Mother did not panic. It was a sad time in our household that night. Tomorrow my special baby brother would be drowned. Mother spent most of the night in prayer. Father sat silence. Aaron and I played with the baby and I cried.

The next morning, Mother insisted that Father go to work. "Maybe, the men will have pity on me alone," she said. So, sorrowfully, Father left. As soon as he was out of the house, Mother became a different person. She told me to run to the worksite nearby and purchase a small amount of pitch or tar. She gave me some coins and a small pail and told me to hurry. When I got back, she took the large straw basket which sat in our home and began covering the inside with that smelly stuff while I cared for Aaron and the baby. "What are you doing?" I asked. "The Lord's will," is all she would say.

Mother worked fast while I tended the baby. The tar hardened quickly since she had put on only a very thin coat. Next, she took a small blanket and double-lined the basket. Then she added the pillow. It was then that I could see what she was doing. Mother nursed him one last time, sang, and rocked him to sleep. Then, I watched in silence as she wrapped her baby in the blankets, placed him in the basket and fastened the basket lid.

"Now, come with me," she said. "We must hurry." Through the back streets toward the Nile, the four of us hurried, Mother carrying the baby in that basket and me with Aaron on my hip. I didn't understand all that was happening, but I did as I was told. We made it through the village without the baby making a sound.

As we approached the Nile, my worst fears were realized. Mother picked a secluded spot where there were no people. She carefully removed the lid and held her child one last time. She let me and Aaron hold him, too. Then, she took him in her arms and blessed him, laid him back in the basket, and covered him once more with the lid.

"Now, what are you going to do?" I asked, already knowing the answer. "Obey Pharaoh and God," she said. "Pharaoh has ordered that we place our child into the Nile and that is what I am doing."

"No! No!' I screamed.

"Hush, now, my child. You must be quiet. For now, we obey God." Then, she explained her plan — God's plan. The child would float safely in the basket on the water until the person of God's own choosing would take him from the water and save his life. It sounded like a risky plan to me. But then, I was only seven years old.

Mother instructed me to get into the water where reeds were growing along the bank. Once I was in the water, she carefully placed the basket next to me. To both of our relief, the basket floated. Then, she told me to push the basket through the reeds and give it a good shove toward the middle of the river where the current would pick it up. Then, I was to quickly make my way back to shore.

I did as I was told, crying all the time. When I got back to Mother, she helped me out of the water, then told me to hurry. I was to run along the bank and keep an eye on the basket. When it came ashore, I was to watch and then do whatever the Lord led me to do. I didn't know what she meant. But she said she couldn't tell me any more plainly because she didn't know what would happen, either. But she assured me that God would not let me down, that when the time came, I would know what to do.

I couldn't stay and argue, for already the current was moving my brother downstream. I had to run to catch up. Can you imagine the burden I felt? If I lost sight of the basket, if I said or did the wrong thing when the basket came ashore, if I did anything wrong, my brother would die!

Sometimes, it was easy to walk along the bank, but sometimes it was necessary for me to leave the bank and climb or detour around obstacles. I was so scared that the basket would be gone out of sight when I got back to the bank. But, each time, the basket was still bobbing along.

We were getting near the place where the Pharaoh had built an outdoor patio with stone steps that led down into the water. Sometimes, in the heat of the day, he and others would sit and relax with their feet in the water. On this day, however, his daughter had come down with her handmaidens and was bathing in the water.

I watched as the basket left the center of the river and floated toward these people, getting caught in the reeds. I sneaked up and got as close as I could and still remain hidden. The princess saw the basket and ordered one of her handmaidens to wade out and get the basket and bring it to her. I watched from the cover of the reeds as she unfastened the lid and looked at my baby brother.

"Oh, how precious," she said. "a baby boy. Isn't he beautiful?" And she picked him up.

"He's a Hebrew baby, your highness," said one of the women. "Put him down, he's dirty."

"Of course, he's dirty," said the Princess, "that's what babies do."

"I didn't mean that," the other woman said. "I mean he belongs to one of those dirty, ignorant, slave people."

"Well, I think he's precious. And I think his mother must be very smart, because she has obeyed my father's command. She did throw him into the Nile. And, I have longed for son. Perhaps, the gods have chosen this way to answer my prayers. Yes, I'll keep him." All this time, I was watching, listening, and praying. I didn't know what to do. I was too little to be doing something this important. How could I know what God wanted me to do?

The woman who was so opposed to the princess keeping the baby said, "You can't keep him because you can't feed him. He'll die without his mother's milk."

Then, I had my answer. Suddenly, I knew exactly what to do. I came out from hiding behind the reeds and walked along, as if by accident. When I came upon the women, I did what any seven-year-old girl would do. I ran up to the princess and began talking and playing with the little boy, my brother!

"Oh, it's so precious. Is it a boy or a girl?

"What do you think?" haughtily answered handmaiden.

"It's a boy," the princess answered.

"What's his name?" I asked.

"Well, let's see," said Pharaoh's daughter. She thought for a moment. "His name is Moses, for I have drawn him from the water." That word "Moses" means "drawn out" in the Egyptian language.

"Are you his mother?" I asked, warming up to this serious game.

"Of course she is not!" said that ugly servant, and an argument ensued among the women. I backed off, uncertain what to do next. But God came through again. I heard the mean woman say, "Even if you tried to keep him, he would die. You can't feed him. Without his mother's milk, he won't live."

Again, I knew just what to do. I sneaked in between them and said to the Pharaoh's daughter, "I know a woman who lost her baby just a couple of days ago. She still has milk. Would you like for me to go and get her for you?"

The princess' face lit up. "Yes, little girl. You go get that woman and bring her to me."

And so I did. I ran as fast as my little legs would let me. I burst into the house and spoke so fast, Mother couldn't understand a word I said. Finally, she calmed me down enough to get the whole story from me. I began pulling on her to get her out the door, but she pulled back. "Hurry," I shouted. "They're waiting."

"First things first," Mother said. And she knelt in prayer and gave thanks to God for her son's deliverance.

When we got back to Pharaoh's patio, the women were still there. I took my mother by the hand and led her up to the princess. I know it must have been hard for Mother not to reach out and embrace her son. Aaron kept reaching for the baby. Thank goodness he didn't talk well enough for Pharaoh's daughter to understand his words.

The princess said to Mother, "The gods have given me this child, a Hebrew boy whom I have named Moses. I want to raise him as my son, but right now he needs a wet nurse. Will you care for him?"

Mother showed remarkable calm. "Yes, my lady," she answered. Then she asked, "Where do you want me to stay?"

The princess thought for a moment, then said, "While he is so young, take him home with you. Bring him to the palace once a day for me to see him. Then, in a few months, when he is older and is beginning to wean, I'll keep him at the palace and you can come in twice a day to feed him."

"Whatever you say," my mother graciously answered. My mother was also a very shrewd woman. "There's just one thing," my mother said. "Since it is against the law for a Hebrew woman to have a boy baby, what if someone finds him and throws him into the river?"

"I hadn't thought of that," the princess answered. "Come with me."

And so Mother, Moses, Aaron and I went to the palace and there Pharaoh's daughter wrote out a special order that no one was to harm the child Moses, grandson of the pharaoh, whom Jochebed, a Hebrew woman, was nursing. Then she sealed the order with her own signet ring. Mother took baby Moses, and the four of us made our way home.

The traitor showed up at our house with soldiers in the afternoon and he had the funniest look on his face when Mother showed him the special protective order of Pharaoh.

When Father returned home that evening, it was clear to see that he was of a heavy heart. "Did Ludim come today?" he fearfully asked.

"Yes!" I shouted. "That nasty man came, but Mother got rid of him real quick!"

Father looked to Mother anxiously. "What happened? Is our baby still alive?"

"He is alive and well," Mother replied, and reached into the sleeping pad, lifted up Moses, and placed in his father's arms.

"How?" Father asked.

"Our God, the God you pray to every day, the God you instruct your people to pray to — to ask for a deliverer, that God has delivered your son. And one day, this child of yours will deliver our people from this terrible slavery."

Then, Mother and I shared the day's events with my father. When the story was ended, Father was humbled, and he led our family in a service of Thanksgiving.

But still, we had to keep our secret. No one could know the child that mother was caring for was, indeed, her own son. For three months Moses lived at home and Mother carried him daily to the palace. Most of the time Aaron and I tagged along. Then, Moses went to live in the palace and Mother would go to nurse him just as Pharaoh's daughter had instructed. Finally, the time came when he was fully weaned. I went with mother that last time. It was hard to say goodbye. Little Moses was so young. He would never remember any of us.

After Moses had been taken to the palace, we shared our story with a few close friends. Most of them didn't believe us. But, a few did. And so, with our family and a few close friends, we kept hope alive, that God — through Moses — would finally deliver his people from bondage.

As the years passed, it seemed as though Moses knew nothing of his Hebrew past. Pharaoh's daughter had been true to her word. She had adopted him. He was schooled in the ways of the Egyptian. His home was in the palace. He had truly become one of the princes of Egypt.

My mother continued to talk of how one day, Moses would deliver our people. Most of the people around us had little hope. Even Father grew tired of her constant claim. One day, he turned really bitterly toward her and said, "How can you believe this? God has abandoned his people. It has been four hundred years and God has left us here. God has forgotten us!"

96

Mother said, "No, oh No! God has *not* forgotten and Moses *will* deliver his people."

"His people! His people!" Father shouted. "He doesn't even know that we *are* his people!"

"Oh, yes," Mother said. "He knows we are his people. He knows that Yahweh is his God. He knows his destiny. He knows he was born to save our people."

"Woman, how can you say such a thing?" Father replied. "We've had no contact with him in all these years, not since he was two years old."

Mother just smiled. And in that quiet, authoritative way of hers, she said, "But he does know. I told him the stories of our people and our God over and over as I carried him in my womb. I told him the stories of our people and our God over and over as I held him in my arms and nursed him. Moses will deliver our people. You will see."

But Father's faith had grown cold. And over the years, it seemed that Father was right. We watched Moses as he grew into a young man. There was never any indication that he knew or cared about his Hebrew heritage.

One day, he witnessed an Egyptian taskmaster severely beating an old Hebrew slave and Moses stepped in to stop it. He pushed the Egyptian, and the Egyptian fell and hit his head. The man was dead. I don't think Moses meant to harm the man, but he panicked and ran.

Now, your writer of the holy scriptures states that Moses was forty years old when this happened. The scripture also states that he stayed away forty years. I don't mean to dispute the sacred writings, but our people sometimes use numbers symbolically. For us to use the number of "forty" symbolizes completion. So, let us just say that in the fullness of time, Moses struck a blow for our freedom and again, in the fullness of time, he returned to complete our deliverance.

Oh, there is so much I could tell you about Moses' encounter with God, about his experience with a bush totally consumed by fire and yet did not burn up, about his return to us in the land of Egypt, about his confrontation with Ramses who had been raised as his brother who was now Pharaoh, about the plagues Moses called down from heaven to force Ramses to release us from bondage, and about that first Passover Night.

But, can you imagine the joy and pride I felt as my baby brother led our people from bondage. I was only sorry that my parents had not lived long enough to see it. But, in a way, Mother did see it. She saw it in her heart. Praise God for mothers like Jochebed to teach us about God from our birth, and who continue to believe in us when no one else does. And praise God that our God is a God who never forgets us nor forsakes us!

Thank you.

MIRIAM

Character: *Miriam — witness to the plagues Moses brought down upon the Egyptians (Interactive)*

Caption: *sister to the Prince Of Egypt*

Publicity Blurb: *"Can you imagine the surprise and the pride as you see your baby brother, that you cast into the Nile, come back many years later and lead your people out of captivity?"*

Scripture: *Exodus 6:1-6*

Responsive Reading: *Canticle of Moses and Miriam (Cantemus Domino)*

Hymns: *"Guide Me, O Thou Great Jehovah;" "Go Down, Moses;" "O Mary, Don't You Weep"*

Scripture Study Prep: *Exodus, Chapter 4:27 – 15:21*

Length of Performance: *word count 3,072*

Dress: *blue robe, blue scarf head drape*

Shoes: *gold sandals*

Accessories: *gold choker, Christmas gold plastic tree garland, Egyptian necklace of Horus, dangling gold earrings, gold bracelets*

Props: *wooden walking stick, wicker basket with cheat sheet hidden inside; tambourine; large ceramic frog, grasshopper, fly (I made), 1 golf ball; 10 small frogs, flies, grasshoppers, ping pong balls; gold letter opener, jeweled chalice, clear glass with dried red food coloring; gold lame cloth, water pitcher*

Make-up: *heavy eye liner, green eye shadow*

Suggested Season to Perform: *Passover*

Miriam

Hello, my name is Miriam, which means strong. My parents knew I had to be strong, because I was born into slavery in Egypt. Our people were not always in Egypt. Six hundred years earlier, our patriarch Abraham of Ur in southern Iraq, migrated with his family into the promised land of Canaan.

During his grandson Jacob's time, a great famine covered our land, forcing Jacob to send two of his sons to Egypt to buy food. When they got there, they found that their brother Joseph had been made prime minister. (Boy, there's a story there!). Joseph brought his father Jacob and all twelve — well eleven — sons to Egypt and the people settled in the land of Goshen up to the north of the city you now call Cairo, up along the shore of the Mediterranean. This was almost two hundred years after Abraham first entered the promised land.

Our people prospered there. We increased in number year-by-year. In time, because of our increase in number, we changed from being respected immigrants to slaves; subtle at first, but growing more severe year-by-year. My father was of the tribe of Levi and, therefore, a priest like his father before him. So, we had things a little easier than many around us, but still we were slaves. My father, as priest, prayed the centuries-old prayer for a deliverer. Our people had been praying that prayer and believing that a deliverer would come, for four hundred years!

As fear of a slave uprising increased, Pharaoh's tactics became more cruel. Finally, the order was issued that all Hebrew male babies be thrown into the Nile River. I was only seven years old when this happened and my mother was pregnant. We kept the pregnancy a secret and prayed and prayed for the baby to be a girl. But no, the baby was a big, beautiful, bouncing baby boy. Have you ever tried to keep an infant quiet?

One day after Father left for work, Mother covered a wicker basket, a lot like this but larger, *(hold up)* with a thin coat of pitch.

She created larger holes in the lid and then wrapped my baby brother in a blanket. *(hold up)* Then Mother, Aaron (he was only three years old at the time), and I took the back roads to the banks of the Nile, to a secluded spot. Mother put me in the water, then handed me the basket and told me to push the basket past the reeds and out into the middle of the river where the current would carry it along and then to rush back to me.

I did as Mother had said, crying all the way. She helped me back up onto the banks and told me to run alongside the river and watch the basket, and when the basket came ashore — to do whatever God led me to do. I asked "What?" She replied, "I don't know, because I don't know what is going to happen. You will just have to rely on God leading you." That's a heavy burden to put on a seven-year-old, but I did as I was told.

I watched as the basket drifted to — I guess you could call it — Pharaoh's recreation spot. There, a seating area was tiled with tile steps leading down into the river. On this day, his daughter was bathing and she saw the basket. She quickly instructed one of her servants to go out and bring the basket to her. I watched and listened as she opened the basket and took out my little brother. Her words amazed me. She said, "Oh, look. I have been praying to the gods for a son and now they have given him to me." One of the servants said, "You can't keep him. First of all, he's a Hebrew baby. They're all supposed to be killed, but also he will die without his mother's milk."

Then I knew what to do. I came out of hiding and walked along and when I got even with the people, I did what any seven-year-old girl would do, I ran up to the baby and took on over him and said "Oh, he's so cute. What's his name?" Pharaoh's daughter thought for a moment and then said, "Well, I guess his name is Moses which means 'drawn from the water' because that's what I did. I drew him from the water."

"Are you his mother?" I asked. "Yes," said Pharaoh's daughter. "No," said the servant girl. Then the servant girl said again, "You can't keep him. I told you, he will die without his mother's milk."

God gave me the words, and I said, "I know a woman who lost her baby just a few days ago. Would you like me to go get her

101

to be a wet nurse for your baby?" Pharaoh's daughter said, "Yes." And so, I ran home as fast as I could to get Mother and bring her to meet the princess. Mother and Pharaoh's daughter came to an agreement. Mother was to nurse young Moses until he was weaned and then turn him over to Pharaoh's daughter. And she did. And Pharaoh's daughter kept her word and Moses grew up in the palace as one of the sons of Egypt.

In the years that followed, Moses seemed to never make any acknowledgment of his Hebrew heritage. But Mother continued to believe that he knew who he was and that one day he would deliver our people. Father did not agree. One day, Moses was out on the construction site where they were working on the pyramids and saw a cruel overseer beating an old man. Without thinking, Moses ran over and attacked the overseer, throwing him to the ground. When the man hit the ground, his head hit a stone, killing him instantly. Then Moses did something I really didn't understand. He ran. He was a prince, he would not have been in trouble. But he did run. And we never saw him again, at least not for forty years.

One day, Moses walked into our home. I knew him instantly. Oh how I wished my mother had lived to see him again. Aaron, who was now the head priest, was not happy to see our brother. "What are you doing here?" he asked. Moses replied, "I'm here to free our people. God told me (Oh, that's a story I could tell about a burning bush), God told me to tell Pharaoh 'Let my people go!'"

Finally, Aaron agreed to help. Together, they went to see Pharaoh, who, at this time, was Ramses, the prince who had been raised as brother to Moses. I followed along behind. Ramses greeted Moses and said, "It's good to see you. What are you doing here?" Moses answered, "My God has told me to come and say to you: 'Let my people go!'" "What?" replied Pharaoh. "And just why would I do that?"

Moses said, "My God is very powerful and he has given me signs and wonders to prove to you that you must let my people go." "Well then, show me some of your signs and wonders." Moses laid his staff down on the ground and the staff turned into a snake. He then picked up the snake by its tail and it was a staff again. Ramses was not impressed. He called for his magicians and they did the same thing. I don't know how any of this happened. I thought it was a miracle from God, but if so, how were his magicians able to do it? Maybe it was some kind of optical illusion.

Moses said again, "Let my people go! Don't make me bring down plagues."

Pharaoh replied, "Oh, I'm so scared. What kind of plague are you going to bring down on me?"

"I'm going to turn the waters of the Nile and all the water in Egypt into *blood*."

"Oh, really?" replied Pharaoh. "This I've got to see."

Moses called for a servant to bring him a pitcher of water. *(Could you bring me a pitcher of water?) (hold up glass with dried dye and pour water into glass)*

When Pharaoh saw this miracle, he was impressed. He said "Okay, the people can go. Now, pray to your God to remove this plague from us." And God changed the blood back into water. But the next day, Pharaoh changed his mind and would not let the people go.

So Moses went back to Pharaoh and said, "Since you have changed your mind, now, if you don't let my people go, God will send down another plague." And suddenly the country was overrun by *frogs*. *(hold up frogs)* There were frogs everywhere. You couldn't walk without stepping on them. They got into the cooking pans, into sleeping pads, and into everything. So Pharaoh called for Moses again and said, "Please, I'll let your people go. Just pray to your God and stop these frogs. And Moses prayed and the frogs went away. At least, the frogs died. People had to scoop them up with shovels and pile them into tall piles. But still, Pharaoh wouldn't let the people go.

Since Pharaoh had gone back on his word, Moses called down another plague. This time it was *gnats*. Tiny little gnats, but they were everywhere. They got into a person's eyes and into their mouth. Moses went again to Pharaoh and the whole scene was replayed. Pharaoh promised to let people go and then changed his mind. So Moses raised his staff and called down another plague. This time it was a plague of *flies*. *(hold up flies)* There were swarms of flies everywhere. And again Pharaoh promised to let the people go. And again Pharaoh went back on his word.

And so Moses called down another plague, and the *animals* in the fields died. And the scene was replayed once more. Then Moses called down yet another plague, this time *boils*. Boils appeared all over every person. (Well, here I need to say that all of these plagues that were occurring all over the country, were not occurring in the land of Goshen where we lived. There was not a single boil on any of the Hebrew people.)

Again the scene played out and Moses called down the seventh plague — *hail*. Hail the size of golf balls *(hold up and drop)* began to fall and crushed the crops in the field. The hail fell so hard and were so large that many people were injured. (throw out ping pong balls into audience) Again Pharaoh promised to let people go and again went back on his word. Moses warned Pharaoh that the plagues were getting more serious. Still Pharaoh's heart was hard. The eighth plague was *locusts*, swarms and swarms of locusts. They destroyed all the crops that were left in the field from the devastating storm of hail. Again, Pharaoh promised and lied and refused to let the people go. (hold up grasshoppers)

The next plague, the ninth, was *darkness*. (*turn off lights*) Moses told Pharaoh that darkness would cover the entire country for three days. And it did. Everywhere except in the land of Goshen. This plague frightened the people more than any of the others. Moses then gave us special instructions. He told us to use these three days to select a lamb from our flock, one without spot or blemish, to slaughter it and smear the blood over the lentils and doorposts of our homes. We were, then, to cook the lamb — roasted, not boiled — to make a dish of bitter herbs to remember the bitterness of our life in slavery; to make a sweet relish of apple or apricot, smashed up with honey and nuts — which looked a little like the mortar used to build the pyramids; and to prepare bread, but not the usual yeast bread but unleavened pita bread. He told us to gather up all of the possessions that we could take with us and be prepared to leave at a moment's notice.

He said that Pharaoh had three days, these three days of darkness, to truly change his heart and let our people go. With a sad heart, Moses said that the tenth and last plague would truly be the most tragic of all. At the end of the three days, Moses went to Pharaoh once more and pleaded with him to change his heart, to let his people go. Again Pharaoh refused. Sadly, Moses pronounced the last final plague that was to befall all of the people of Egypt. That was the *death of every firstborn* person in every house. Pharaoh seemed nervous, but still refused to let the people go.

As Moses left the palace, he sent word to us to hurriedly eat our special meal — to eat the meal with our coats and shoes on and be ready to leave as soon as Moses gave the signal. That night as we ate that special symbolic meal, we began to hear the cries of our Egyptian neighbors. And hearing their wails, we realized that the last plague had occurred. That night, the angel of death *passed over* every home and killed the first born in every home where the *blood of the lamb* was not applied.

Moses went once again to the palace to stand before Pharaoh. Pharaoh was sitting on his throne holding his dead son in his arms. Pharaoh was finally a broken man. He told Moses that Moses and his God had won, for Moses to take his people and leave his land and never come back.

As Moses left, he blew the shofar as a signal to our people to grab our possessions and leave. As we started out of town, the Egyptian neighbors came out and gave us gifts of *gold* — (hold up items in basket) gold ropes like this and earrings and bracelets; necklaces like this Horus, the falcon God. The main duty of this god was to protect the Pharaoh, which clearly he had not done. We were also given goblets, gold clothing. The people were afraid of us and our God. We took their wealth — we plundered the Egyptians.

Moses led us through the city and out into the country. Then for the next few days, we were led by a pillar of clouds by day and a pillar of fire by night. Finally, we arrived at the Red Sea. We didn't know where to go next. Should we turn to the right or to the left? Then, someone saw a cloud of dust behind us. As we watched that cloud grow nearer, we could make out that it was dust thrown up by the army of Pharaoh's chariots. One of the men in our group shouted to Moses, "Weren't there enough graves for us in Egypt? Did you have to bring us out here for a watery grave?"

Moses stood on the banks of the Red Sea and raised his staff once again. (*hold up staff*) "*Do not be afraid, stand firm and see the deliverance that the Lord will accomplish for you today; for the Egyptians whom you see today, you shall never see again. The Lord will fight for you, and you have only to keep still.*" As he spoke these words, a strong wind rose up blowing upon the waters. The wind blew the waters in opposite directions, creating a path in between. Even though the soldiers were drawing nearer, Moses continued to stand with his staff raised and the wind continued to blow. When night approached, the pillar of clouds that had led us, moved behind us, separating us from the oncoming chariots. That night there was no pillar of fire. The soldiers were forced to stop their approach until daylight. All night Moses stood and held his staff upward toward God, at times needing assistance from Aaron and his friend Hur to keep his hand raised.

All night, the wind blew. By morning, the wind had dried the land on that path between the waters. Moses, then, gave the command for all of us to cross over to the other side by walking through that water. It was frightening. No one wanted to do it. The walls, twenty or thirty feet high, lined the path on each side. Finally, I took the lead and encouraged the people to make the crossing. And the walls of water held until we all crossed over.

Then Moses turned, still holding his staff in his hand, and waited until all of Pharaoh's army were in the midst of that dry path. Then he dropped his staff and the walls of water collapsed on the army. It was terrible. We could hear the men screaming. We could hear the horses, who were also panicked. Then, in just a short time, all was quiet and we could see the bodies of the horses and the riders floating on the water.

Moses then led our people in a prayer of thanksgiving to God for our deliverance. But I was so full of excitement and praise, that simply listening to Moses offer a prayer was not enough for me. I grabbed my tambourine (*take up tambourine*) and led the women and children in song and dance. I sang:

"Praise be to Yahweh / mighty is he / horse and rider / hath he thrown into the sea."

Over and over, the more we sang, the louder we got. And the louder we got, the faster we sang and the faster we danced. Let's all give it a try. Let's make a circle and move around singing. *(lead group) "Praise be to Yahweh / mighty is he / horse and rider hath he thrown into the sea." "Praise be to Yahweh / mighty is he / horse and rider hath he thrown into the sea."* (— sing it with me) over and over — faster and faster —

Finally, I fell exhausted on the ground. Oh yes, I was exhausted — but it was a good exhaustion. Praise and joy welled up in me and I shouted: *(hands raised)*

Free at last; free at last. Thank God almighty, we are free at last!

Thank you for letting me share my memories of the first Passover with you — that great exodus out of bondage. Thank you.

ESTHER

Character: *Esther*

Caption: *Beauty Queen With A Dangerous Secret*

Publicity Blurb: *"How would you feel if, by speaking out, you might prevent genocide; but by speaking out, you might lose your life?"*

Hymns: *"Stand Up, Stand Up for Jesus;" "Through It All;" by Andrea Crouch*

Scripture Read: *Esther 4:14; Psalm 27:1,2,6*

Scripture Study Prep: *the Book of Esther*

Length of Performance: *word count 5,176*

Dress: *floor-length brown, strapless, tube knit dress with gold lame wrap*

Shoes: *gold, "bedroom-type" slippers*

Accessories: *long, dangling gold earrings; gaudy gold bracelets; gold ring; long "rope" of gold plastic Christmas tree garland; large gold choker*

Hair: *hair washed, not coiffured, and curled into very tight curls — not combed out, with gold "cloth" like headband with square-colored "gems" glued on, worn across forehead, not in hair*

Make-up: *heavy eye liner with dark green eye shadow*

Props: *scepter from party supply store; plastic gold and silver goblets from party store with gems glued on; made-up scroll; mention of box-office movie "One Night With The King" starring Tiffany Dupont, John Rhyes Davies, Omar Sharif, and Peter O'Toole (2006)*

Suggested Season to Perform: *Purim*

Esther

Beauty Queen With A Dangerous Secret

Hello, my name is Esther, at least, that is the name you know me by. "Esther" is my Persian name. "Hadassah" is my real name, the name given to me by my mother and father. I hated that name "Esther" because it was a reference to the goddess Ishtar, who was worshiped by the Persian people. My name, "Hadassah" means "myrtle," a bush whose leaves are fragrant only when crushed. I want to thank you for inviting me here today.

I am of the Jewish faith and the Jewish race. My country of Judah had been captured by King Nebuchadnezzar and my people — not everybody — but a large number of our people had been carried off to their land, Babylon in modern day Iran, in what was later to be called the Babylonian Exile. Eventually, Nebuchadnezzar was defeated by the Persian King Cyrus. Cyrus allowed our people to return to our homeland, but many chose to stay in Persia, even though the Persian people didn't like our people very much. My family had chosen to stay in Persia. Most of us looked very similar to the other people in that land, so if the person did not know that we were Jewish, there seemed no reason to tell them.

Let me tell you how this story began. Xerxes was the king. And for a number of years, things had been going very well. He was very prosperous. Peace reigned. So, he declared a time of celebration. For six months the palace there in Susa — which was usually restricted to only the royal family and entourage and a very few invited guests — for six months the governors, their aides, the military leaders, and the civic leaders in all the 127 provinces were invited to this continuous celebration. Everything was elaborate. The bunting of blue, green, and white was draped from pillar to pillar by cords of fine purple linen fastened to large silver rings. Couches covered in gold and silver had been placed in the courtyard, which was paved with white marble, red feldspar, shining mother-of-pearl, and blue turquoise.

There were different parties each night. There were tumbling acts, musical shows, even a production of Euripides' latest play.

Xerxes himself, gave stirring dramatic readings from Homer's Iliad and Odyssey. And, of course, there were the usual belly dancers.

Royal wine flowed in abundance. All guests were served the wine in exquisite goblets of gold and silver. Xerxes prided himself in the fact that no two goblets were exactly alike. His only restriction on the wine was that no one should be compelled to take more than he wanted. For six months the celebrations continued. Xerxes was really showing off how benevolent he was.

And then, Xerxes did something very unusual. He declared a week-long event and opened the celebration to the palace servants and workers, everyone from secretaries to janitors. While all these last parties were going on, (and of course, they were for men only, except for the showgirls and the "women of the night"), the women were having their own party over at the queen's wing of the palace. Toward the end of this week of celebration, the king decided to show off his beautiful queen. He was convinced that Vashti was the most beautiful woman in the kingdom.

Most of the lower officials had not had an opportunity to see her up close. So he called for his eunuch and sent an order to Vashti for her to appear before him in the best of her royal robes, complete with crown. The eunuch delivered the summons. I was told later by someone who was present what happened when the queen received this message. The servant announced to Vashti that the king had ordered her presence immediately, as soon as she was properly attired.

Vashti then shocked everyone at the party. She looked at the eunuch and said, "No! Tell the king I'm busy with a party of my own. It is not convenient for me to come at this time."

Well, she may have been the queen, but *nobody* turns down the king's order. Her handmaids rushed to her side, urging her to reconsider.

"I don't have to worry about anything," she said. "Xerxes is so crazy about me that I can do virtually anything I want and get away with it. I'm not in any danger. He may be a king, but underneath those robes, he's just a man like anyone else. I've got him wrapped around my little finger."

110

So, she signaled the musicians to continue playing and the party continued. The eunuch was very nervous about delivering that message, because this was back in the time when the messenger could be beheaded simply for bringing bad news.

When the eunuch returned to the king, he spoke softly. "Speak up!" the king shouted. "I can't hear you. How soon before she arrives?"

"I'm sorry, my Lord," the eunuch replied, "but she will not be coming."

"What do you mean, she won't be coming?"

"I gave her your message, and she said to tell you that she was busy with a party of her own."

"She *what*?" He shouted so loudly that everyone around stopped to listen. "Did you tell her it was an order from me?"

"Yes."

"And she still refused?"

"Yes, my Lord."

Three of the king's court advisors, lawyers really, came up and asked, "What's wrong?"

Xerxes told them what had happened. "She refused to come! She embarrassed me in front of my guests. Now what am I going to do?"

Two of the advisors hem-hawed a little, but the third was bold. "You know, this is really very serious. She has disrespected you. She has disobeyed her husband, even if she is the queen. This could have far-reaching implications. All the women there at her party already know what has happened. As soon as these men arrive at home tonight, they will be told what happened: that the queen doesn't obey her husband. There will be revolution in every home. Our wives will no longer obey us. It will be utter chaos!"

"I know, I know," replied the king. "But what am I to do?"

"I tell you what I think would be wise," continued his advisor. "Right now, I would issue an order banishing Vashti, not only from the palace, but from the country as well! Effective immediately! Today! All our wives have got to know that they cannot disobey their husbands and get away with it. They must know that the man is in charge. The man rules the house. And if they defy that simple fact, their punishment will be harsh and swift."

"Yes, yes, you're right. That's what I'll do. I'll banish her. Take care of it for me, will you?"

"As you wish, my Lord."

The king dismissed himself from the party and returned to his quarters. Meanwhile, back at Vashti's party, there was a damper on the festivities. Suddenly, the king's advisor and four of the king's guards appeared. "By order of the king, you are no longer queen of this land. You are hereby banished from this kingdom, effective immediately!"

Before Vashti could utter a protest, the guards seized her and began dragging her out of the room. "Wait", cried one of her handmaidens, "Let me gather a few of her things together."

"She won't need them where she's going," he replied.

With that remark, Vashti and the guards disappeared. Her handmaids knew what the advisor meant. Vasthi was never seen or heard from again.

Xerxes was now left without a queen. For a little while that did not bother him, after all he had a whole harem. But when he got over being drunk and being mad, he missed Vashti. He called his advisers again and said, "I'm lonely. It's not good for king not to have a queen. But I don't know who to pick."

Again, his advisers had just the answer for him. They suggested that he conduct a massive, kingdom-wide beauty contest. The prettiest woman from each province would be brought to the palace. After they were "prettied up", the king would meet them one by one and make his selection. He could take as long as he wanted. It might be hard, but he sure would enjoy the work.

The king thought that sounded like a good idea. So, the decree was issued. Until the first crop of beauties arrived, Xerxes entertained himself with the women in his harem. The bulletin went out throughout the land. The king was desiring a new queen, one to be chosen from the most beautiful women of the land.

I was a young woman of fifteen years at this time. I had been orphaned very young, and my uncle Mordecai had taken me and raised me as his own child. As I said, I was Jewish, but I was also beautiful. I'm not bragging, just stating facts.

Mordecai was a good man and he was very smart. He liked to cover as many bases as possible. He figured that for his adopted daughter to become queen, that wouldn't be such a bad idea. So, he entered me in this regal beauty contest.

I was horrified when he came home and told me what he had done. I didn't think I could win. What if I did? The last thing I wanted as a young Jewish girl was to be married to that old anti-Semitic man, even if he was the king.

Well, as luck would have it, I won. I won in my hometown. I won in the district. I won all the way up to my province, which meant that I was one of a select group who actually made it all the way to the palace there in Susa.

I didn't see the king except at a great distance. For six months, I underwent special beauty treatments. I had been a common laborer, so my hands and my skin were dry and rough. I soaked in milk baths, then perfumed water until I thought I would shrivel into nothingness. But the baths softened my skin and even lightened it a little.

My coarse hair was treated with hot oils and coiffured into the latest style. I was taught how to walk, how to talk, what silverware to use at fancy government dinners. I was also taught how to please a man. You see, I was a virgin. I hadn't even dated but a few times. I was so naïve. But the wiser women instructed me how to behave when the king called for me. It was embarrassing, but it was information I needed to know.

The routine the king had worked out was that each night, he would send for a different girl. After dinner in his quarters, she would entertain him with whatever talent she possessed; singing or whatever. Then they would go to bed. He might be mildly impressed if she was intelligent. But the truth was that the king was only interested in two things; how beautiful she was and how good she was in bed. After that one night together, the girl went to the official king's harem, since she had slept with the

113

king. He might never call her again unless he had been especially impressed by her, remembered her name or asked for her again. Otherwise, she would live out her life locked into the harem wing of the palace, guarded over by eunuchs.

I decided that given the options, it was clearly to my advantage to win the king's favor. I soaked, I studied, I listened. Finally, my night came. I was so nervous. I had never met the king before. I had never slept with a man before. My whole future was on the line, and with a man I had never met, a man who cared nothing for me.

The head eunuch had taken a particular liking to me and saved out the most beautiful gown for me to wear. The servants dressed me and fixed my hair. My eyes were made up to perfection. I looked good.

I took a deep breath and then was led off to see the king. He was immediately impressed. He liked the way I looked, he liked my singing, and my conversation. I won't go into detail on what happened later during the evening, but by morning, he had decided that this was the one. I would be his queen!

I was crowned queen of Persia. At official state functions, I would sit beside him and look pretty. Now, I still didn't live with him. I had an apartment in a different section of the palace and visited him only when sent for. Sometimes, that would be every night in a row for several weeks. But, sometimes, several weeks would pass without seeing him. It was whatever the king desired. But I could not go to him at any time, for any reason, on my own. I had to wait for him to summon me. If I had tried to enter his bed chamber or the throne room uninvited, I would have been banished, or worse.

During this time, my uncle Mordecai had moved into town and secured a low-level job there in the palace. He would check on me, sending messages to me through a eunuch or servant. The servants all knew him and liked him.

One day, Mordecai overheard two of the king's servants talking. They felt that they had been treated unjustly. They had decided to assassinate the king. My uncle listened very carefully and heard the details. As soon as they had gone, he scrawled out an urgent message to me, telling me of the plot and gave it to the eunuch who watched over me. I immediately got word to Xerxes by a servant telling him of Mordecai's information. There was an investigation and the men were arrested and hanged.

For the next several years, I reigned as queen. And, I have to admit, it wasn't a bad life. Now, nobody knew that I was Jewish. My uncle had insisted that I keep that a secret. And no one knew that Mordecai was my uncle. Some knew that he befriended me, knew that there was some kind of connection. But no one knew he was my father's brother.

Then, my husband appointed as prime minister, a positively horrid, ambitious man by the name of Haman. Xerxes ordered all the subjects to bow and kneel as he walked by as a sign of respect. Well, the people knew better than to defy the king, regardless of what they thought of nasty old Haman — all that is, except my uncle. He refused to bow.

Haman noticed this flagrant disobedience and questioned Mordecai. My uncle replied, "I am a Jew, and I bow to no one but the one true God." Haman was outraged. Every other person bowed. But that wasn't enough. Mordecai's defiance galled him, robbed him of the joy of his new position. Haman saw his chance to get rid of, not only Mordecai, but of all those nasty Jews whom he detested so much. He was in power now. People had to do as he ordered.

He went to Xerxes. "My Lord, there are some people in this land, some of your subjects, who are really your enemies. You need to rid your land of these people."

"Who are you talking about?" asked my husband.

"The Jews, sire."

"The Jews? I don't see a problem? They're good, hard-workers. They obey orders. They've never given me any trouble."

"That's just because you don't know them like I do," replied Haman. "They refuse to bow to us, saying that they pledge allegiance to only one — to their God. Believe me, you need to get rid of them. You need to issue a law, the Law of the Medes and Persians, that on a certain day of the year, (you can roll the dice to pick the day), on that day, the good people of this land are to go out and slaughter the enemy Jews. And, any enemy they kill, they can confiscate their property."

Xerxes wasn't convinced. "Think of all the expense a campaign like that would incur — issuing bulletins, carrying out all this. No, I don't think it would be worth it."

But Haman wouldn't let it drop. "My Lord, it would be my pleasure to finance this purge."

"Well, okay. If you feel that strongly about it and you're willing to pay for it, go ahead." My husband took off his ring and gave it to Haman to use to fix the royal seal when he sent out the royal decree.

Haman lost no time in getting the order issued. In February of the following year, all the Jews in the country were to be killed. It would be the greatest holocaust the world had ever seen. When my uncle heard of this order, he ripped his clothing, put on a sackcloth, scooped up dirt and heaped it upon his head. That is our Jewish ritual for mourning.

One of my maidservants saw Mordecai dressed like that, sitting at the gate of the palace. She told me, and not knowing what had happened, I sent out clean clothes for him. Mordecai refused the clothes, so I sent the head eunuch out to find out what was going on. He returned with Mordecai's story and a copy of the king's decree.

I was horrified. I could not believe that I was married to a man who could do such a thing. The eunuch then produced a note from my uncle. In it, he asked me to go to Xerxes and plead for our people.

I sent a note back to my uncle. "My dear uncle, I cannot do as you ask. If anyone, man or woman, unsummoned enters the inner court room to see the king, that person must die. The only exception is if the king raises and extends his golden scepter. Xerxes has not sent for me in over a month. It is too dangerous."

Mordecai sent back a scathing message. *"My dear child, don't imagine that you are safer than any other Jew just because you are in the royal palace. If you keep quiet at a time like this, help will come from heaven to the Jews, and they will be saved; but you will surely die. Yet, who knows, maybe it was for a time like*

116

this that you were made queen! Go to the king, confess that you are Jewish and plead our case."

When I received that reply, I knew what I had to do. I sent one last message to my uncle. "Go and get all the Jews in Susa together, hold a fast and pray for me. Don't eat or drink anything for three days and nights. My servant girls and I will be doing the same. After that, I will go to the king, even though it is against the law. If I must die for doing it, then I will die."

Upon receiving my note, my uncle set out to organize the Jews of the city, and I began my fast. For three days I stayed in prayer, praying, pleading for the fate of my people. On the third day, I bathed, put on my royal robes, fixed my hair the way I knew Xerxes liked it, and headed toward Xerxes' inner court. At the door, I paused momentarily, offered one last prayer, and stepped inside. Xerxes was sitting on the royal throne. He looked up and saw me. I held my breath. Then I saw his golden scepter. He held it out to me and said in a very cheerful voice, "What is it, Esther? Tell me what you want. You shall have it, even if it is half my kingdom."

Luck, or God, was with me. I had caught him on a good day. But I knew I had to play this smart. So I said, "It would please me greatly, my husband, if you and Haman would be my guests tonight, at a special dinner I have prepared for you."

My husband agreed and sent word for Haman to join him at my quarters. Over the wine, my husband asked me again, "Now, tell me what you want and you can have it. I will grant your request, even if you ask for half my kingdom."

I played the stupid game with him a little longer. I smiled and said, "If your majesty will grant my request, I would like for you and Haman to be my guests again tomorrow night for another special dinner. At that time I promise I will tell you what I want."

You could tell Haman was really happy when he left my place. He had finally made it with the "in" crowd. But as he left the palace, he saw my uncle sitting there in dirt and ashes and again Mordecai did not rise, bow, or show any sign of respect. Haman was furious. All the joy he had experienced at dinner was now gone.

I understand that when he got home, he really lost it. He ranted and raved about how important he was now and how everyone was bowing to him, everybody but Mordecai. And yet, he said, none of this meant anything to him when he saw Mordecai sitting at the entrance of the palace. "I can't wait for him to get what's due him," he said.

One of his friends made a good point. "Well, why do you have to wait? You're in power now. You can do what you want. Why don't you hang that son-of-a-gun?"

Haman liked that idea. So he decided to head back to the palace right then, in the middle of the night, to give orders to have a giant gallows built and ready for use by morning. He would hang Mordecai high, and then he would come to my place for dinner with me and the king. Oh, he would be in high spirits that night!

Now, it just so happened that on that same night, my husband could not get to sleep. So, he had the official records of the kingdom brought in and read to him. If you don't think that will put you to sleep, you haven't read our chronicles. The part read to him that night included the account how Mordecai had uncovered a plot to assassinate him. Xerxes interrupted the scribe and asked, "By the way, how did we honor Mordecai for doing that?"

His servant was a little timid when he replied, "Sir, I don't think you did anything for him."

"Well, it's high time we did," my husband replied. "Are there any of my officials in the palace now?"

It was the middle of the night and the servant doubted that there were any officials around, but he went out and checked. He came back and reported that Haman was in the palace.

"Good. Good. Haman is just the one. Bring him here."

Haman was so glad that he just happened to be in the palace when the king needed him. Things were really beginning to go his way. Xerxes said, "Haman, there is someone I wish very much to honor. I need advice on what to do for this man."

Haman thought to himself, "Surely the man the king wishes to honor is me." He thought for a moment. "Here is what I think would be a good way to show that you honor this man. Have royal robes brought this man, robes that you yourself have worn. Put the royal ornaments on your horse. Then have one of your men dress this man, mount him on your horse, and lead him through the city square and have the man cry out, 'See how the king rewards those he wishes to honor.'"

Xerxes thought for a moment and then said, "Yes, that sounds like a good idea. Okay, Haman, go get the robes and get everything ready for tomorrow morning, for this is what I want to do to honor Mordecai. And you will be the one to lead the horse and cry out for me."

Haman was outraged! Honoring Mordecai! What could the king be thinking of? He was seething, but he held his anger until he left the king's sight. When morning came, he did as the king had instructed. Then Haman hurried home, totally humiliated. He told his wife everything that had happened. She was not very sympathetic. "Seems to me like you're letting that Jew get the best of you," she replied. Haman didn't know what to do. About that time, the coachman arrived to carry him to my banquet.

Well, I put a big spread before them again, even fancier than the night before. I served the best wine in the kingdom. I was my most adorable, most charming self. When the meal was over, Xerxes started the little game again. "Now, my queen, tell me what you want. I'll give it to you, even if it's half my kingdom."

Now was the time. I took a deep breath, uttered a silent prayer, and jumped right into it. "If it would please your majesty to grant my humble request, my wish is that I *might live*, and that my people might live. My people and I have been sold for slaughter. If it were nothing more serious than being sold into slavery, I could have kept quiet and not bothered you about it. But we are about to be destroyed. Exterminated!"

"What? Who dares to do this? Where is the man who would do such a thing!"

I raised myself to my full queenly height, pointed my finger straight into the face of Haman and in a strong, steady voice said, "That evil man, Haman. He is the one doing this!"

"No! No!" shouted Haman. "It's those terrible Jews who are the target of that day of slaughter."

"I, sir, am a Jew!"

All color left Haman's face, a look of sheer terror in his eyes. Xerxes jumped up in a fury. He stomped out the patio doors and marched up and down the garden, venting his anger with ungodly expletives. I could see that Haman knew that his time was up. He knew that he would be severely punished. And so, all of a sudden, he tried to play up to me, play on my sympathy; to beg me to intercede for him. I had just sat down on the couch and as he came over to kneel at my feet, his foot slipped and he stumbled and landed right on top of me, just as my husband walked in from the garden.

"Is this man going to rape my queen right here in front of me, in my own palace?" my husband shouted. He immediately called for the guards, ordered Haman to be carried out to be executed. As Haman was being led off, one of the guards said, more or less under his breath, but loud enough for Xerxes to hear, "Just think, he was just down here in the middle of the night having a gallows built to hang Mordecai on."

"What is this?" asked my husband.

The servant told him about Haman's elaborate plan to hang Mordecai on the biggest gallows ever built.

"Then, hang Haman from it!" commanded the king. So Haman was dragged off and hanged on the gallows he had built for Mordecai.

Well, all this intrigue was well and good. And I was certainly glad to see Haman get what was due him. But it didn't change our fate one little bit. So, later that day, when my husband had had time to cool down, it was necessary for me to go to him again. To make restitution to me, my husband granted all the property belonging to Haman. I was now a wealthy woman in my own rights. I told my husband my whole life story, including the truth that Mordecai was my uncle, actually my adoptive father. I broke down crying and fell at his feet and begged him to stop that evil plot that Haman had set into motion, that order to kill, to eradicate the Jewish people.

My husband was touched. "But what can I do? You know the law of the Medes and Persians cannot be revoked. That law must stand." Then, I had an idea. "I don't know what he can do, but my uncle is a very smart man and a man who goes to our God for guidance. Maybe he can think of something."

Xerxes sent for Mordecai. He said, "I don't know exactly how you can do it. I can't revoke the law, but maybe you can come up with a law to counter it. Here's my ring. Good luck."

My uncle lost no time. He called in the king's secretaries and dictated letters to the Jews, the governors, to the administrators in all of the 127 provinces all the way from Egypt to the Sudan. The letters were written to each province in their own language so there could be no mistake of its intent. These letters explained that the king would allow the Jews in every city to organize for self-defense and encouraged the Jewish people to defend themselves. And it further stated that they, the Jews, could claim the possessions of any Persians they defeated.

There was great relief in the city of Susa that night. And yet, there was also great danger facing us. When that horrible day came, it was a blood bath everywhere on both sides. Thousands of people were killed. But the end result was that our people, the Jewish people, were triumphant.

Throughout the kingdom, the day became a great day of victory. The day after the massacre became a great day of celebration for the Jewish people. Mordecai had these events written down and letters were sent throughout the Persian empire, declaring that day as a day of celebration for generations to come in memory of our great victory, and a remembrance of how God had brought triumph from immediate, imminent destruction. This day is celebrated still, even in your time. It is held the first week in March and is called the Festival of Purim, "purim" meaning "dice", because the date of that fateful day was decided by the roll of the dice.

I served by my husband's side for many years. My uncle Mordecai was promoted to second-in-command throughout the kingdom.

Though times can be hard, though it may look like all is against you, though you may be asked to do what you feel you do not have the strength to do, through it all — through it all, I've learned that you can depend on God!

Thank you.

MARY MAGDALENE

Character: *Mary Magdalene*

Caption: *The First Apostle*

Publicity Blurb: *"Can you imagine the joy of being the first one ever to see our risen Lord?"*

Scripture: *Matthew 16:9-11*

Hymns: *"Up From The Grave He Arose;" "In The Garden;" "We've A Story To Tell To The Nations"*

Scripture Study Prep: *last chapters of the gospels*

Length of Performance: *word count 3, 641*

Dress: *dusty pink robe; head drape*

Shoes: *biblical sandals*

Accessories: *"oriental" jewelry, gold ring and belt*

Props: *none*

Make-up: *usual*

Suggested Season to Perform: *Eastertide; Evangelism or Missions emphasis or last portion at outdoor Easter Sunrise Service*

Mary Magdalene

The First Apostle

Hello. Thank you for inviting me here to tell you my story. My name is Mary. Of course, a lot of women in my day were named Mary. I am called Mary Magdalene because I come from the fishing village of Magdella, four miles north of Tiberias along the Sea of Galilee. I had a good childhood. My father had made a good living in the fishing industry. We attended sabbath services each week at the synagogue.

But, as I grew older, I grew dissatisfied with my life. The whole town smelled of fish. I resented having to go to church every week. I became rebellious. And, as soon as I was old enough, I left home for the big city. I never became a woman of ill repute, but I came close — a real rebel. It was almost like I suffered from a sickness of the mind. I was a profoundly unhappy person, into destructive habits, destructive lifestyle. I heard people speak of a young rabbi who taught on the hillsides and taught with great authority and wisdom. This was early in his ministry, but so many people were already talking about him, I decided to go and see and hear for myself.

There was a large crowd gathered and I had to stand at the back. But amazingly, I could still hear his words clearly. His stories were marvelous. His teachings were powerful, but they differed from the rabbis that I had heard before with his emphases on love. For instance, at one point, Jesus quoted from our holy scriptures. He said, "It has been said 'an eye for an eye, a tooth for a tooth' but I say unto you to *love* your enemies, bless them that curse you, do good to them that hate you." Love your enemies? That was something different. It made me want to hear more, but the time of his teaching was ending.

As the crowd dispersed, I was able to get closer to Jesus. His back was to me and I could see nothing of his appearance, except that he was very tall. "Oh, turn around," I thought. "Please turn around." I can usually judge a man if I can look him in the eye.

Just then, as if Jesus heard my thoughts, he turned around and looked me straight in the eye. It was as though there were no other people in the world — only the two of us. As I "turned my eyes upon Jesus and looked full in his wonderful face, the things of earth grew strangely dim in the light of his glory and grace." He looked deep into my soul and I felt all pretense, all bitterness, all fear dissolve in his gaze. I fell on my knees before him, and he laid his hand lightly upon my head and in a soft voice, yet full of authority, said, "Demons, leave this woman."

I don't know quite how to explain it, but I felt clean on the inside. I felt *whole*. I knew, in an instant, that God loved me. And I knew, also, that I would follow this man, Jesus, to the ends of the earth. Oh, I wanted so badly to be one of his disciples. But, of course, I couldn't be a real disciple, because only men were disciples. But I've never known a man, much less a group of men, who didn't need a little help from a woman. I decided to be that woman; to support him with cooking and cleaning, to support him financially (for I did have money). And, I was willing to stay in the background, to stay at his side, doing whatever I could for him and his mission.

For almost three years, I traveled with Jesus. I worked. Oh, I worked. I cooked and cleaned and mended, but I also learned. And so, I guess I did become a disciple after all — for that's what a disciple is — one who sits and learns from the Master. Not only did I hear the teachings, the stories, the parables that he taught to the crowds — but I was privileged to hear the private explanations that he gave his "inner circle."

Those three years were wonderful. The teachings and stories were powerful. And the signs and wonders that followed him were proof that Jesus was indeed the Son of God. I saw miracles performed almost daily. I saw a multitude of people fed from only a few loaves and fishes. I saw the lame walk, the blind see, the lepers cured. And, perhaps even more importantly for me personally, I saw those who were depressed, those who were possessed, healed.

His ministry appealed to all types of people. There were some in the crowds who were wealthy, those of high political and social standing, some even members of the Sanhedrin. But, there were many more who were poor. The time with Jesus was exciting. But, the best of all was just being in his presence. During this time, I caught his vision of peace on earth — of God's kingdom becoming a reality — right here, right now.

As the time of Passover grew near, I detected an inner conflict in Jesus. On the one hand, he was excited about celebrating the religious holiday in Jerusalem, as was his custom. Yet, on the other hand, he seemed hesitant to make the journey. In the end, he decided to go to Jerusalem as he had every year.

As we neared the city men, women, and children greeted us with shouts of praise. "Hosanna, blessed is he who comes in the name of the Lord." The children waved palm branches. The men lay down their cloaks before Jesus. I was so proud. My heart nearly burst within me. Finally, Jesus was getting the praise and recognition he deserved.

Jesus had made the decision to observe the tradition Passover meal, the seder, on Thursday night — the last night of the week-long celebration, as was the tradition. Now, the seder is a very elaborate meal with each element symbolizing events surrounding that first Passover when the angel of death "passed over" the homes of the Hebrew people and saved all those inside whose homes had been covered by the blood of the lamb. It was decided to hold this meal in the upstairs room of a believer who lived on Mount Zion, not far from the temple. And so, we went to his home to finalize the plans.

Since I could not sit at table with the men, I offered my assistance to the woman of the house for the preparation of the meal. As I said, the meal was very elaborate and time-consuming. Each element stood for some special event in the lives of the slaves in bondage in Egypt. Of course, the slain lamb — the sacrificial lamb — was the centerpiece of the meal. There was parsley dipped in salt water to remind the people of the saltiness of the tears shed. Horseradish or other bitter herbs reminded them of the bitter hardships they had endured. Even the dessert, made of crushed apples and nuts, reminded them of the mortar they had used as they were forced to build the pyramids.

On Thursday morning, I arrived at the home ready to work. And, we did work — all day long. I made many trips up and down those outer stairs. Toward evening, the men began arriving. On one of my trips upstairs, I was surprised to see Jesus, his outer robe removed, wearing his under-tunic and a towel wrapped around his waist, actually kneeling and washing his disciples' feet, clearly, the act of a servant. I lingered near the door and I heard him say, "As I have washed your feet, so you ought to wash one another's feet."[12]

Finally, the meal was prepared and the meal was served. After the meal, the men sang one of the psalms traditionally used for Passover. Then, the men dispersed — Jesus and three of his closest friends over to the Mount of Olives, to the Garden of Gethsemane to pray. I'm not sure where the other men went. I stayed at the home until all the dishes were washed, dried and put away and the furniture was all put back in place. Then I too, left to spend the night with relatives in the city.

The next day, I learned of the arrest, the night trial, the appearance before Pilate — and the verdict! I ran through the streets panic–driven. I arrived at Golgotha, the Place of the Skull in time to see Jesus lying on the ground on top of the cross. And the soldiers driving stakes through our Lord's hands and feet.

At this sight, I became sick to my stomach and went off to the side to throw up. Then, I took my place at the foot of the cross to stand vigil until his suffering in this world was over. His mother, several other women and John joined me. No Peter, no Andrew, or James or Judas. Of all his trusted disciples, only John had the guts to show up at his death.

Crucifixion can sometimes last for days. Mercifully, Jesus' death came in a matter of hours. As his body was lowered from the cross, two wealthy men, Joseph of Arimathea and Nicodemus, a Pharisee, a member of the Sanhedrin, received the body and loosely covered his body with a cloth they found lying about. John and I supported his mother as Joseph led the tiny funeral procession to a tomb in Joseph's nearby garden. Gently, they laid the body of Jesus on a hewn-out slab. But there was no time to

12 The word "ought" is from the Latin "mandatum"(mandate), giving the term "Maundy" Thursday in remembrance of this event.

prepare his body for burial, even if we had had the oil and spices with us.

Sundown was fast approaching. And not just any sundown, but the sundown ushering in the sabbath, and our religion did not allow us to be out or to travel on the sabbath. So, we had no choice but to leave his bloodied body there with plans to return as soon as possible after sabbath had ended.

All day Saturday, Joanna, several other women and I sat with his mother. We could not begin the official time of mourning, or *sit shiva* until the body had been properly prepared for burial. Then, we would begin wailing out our grief in the traditional manner. So, we sat in silence. I was nearly numb with grief and confusion. I truly believed that Jesus was the Son of God. But, you can't kill God — can you?

When the sabbath was over, we began gathering the spices and linens we would need to properly prepare the body for burial. Of course, we had plenty of oil and linens. But, we didn't have nearly enough of the burial spices. One does not usually keep a large quantity of those burial spices in the home. And, of course, we had had no reason to think we would need them. It was decided that two of the women would leave to buy the spices the next morning, as soon as the stores were open, and then meet us at the tomb.

Before I went to bed, I pulled Joanna aside and spoke to her. "Do you remember the condition of our Lord's body when we left him in that tomb?"

"Of course, I do," she replied. "It was horrible. There was so much blood, in his beard, his hair, and that terrible gash on his side."

"Joanna, I can't bear for his mother to see his body in that shape. Let's go early, before the others, and wash as much blood off his body as possible. Let's make his 'body' as presentable as we can."

She agreed. And, so, about an hour before daybreak, Joanna and I left for the tomb each carrying a pail of water and some cleaning rags. Mary would come later to ceremoniously wash his body and anoint it with oil and spices, and wrap the body in fresh linens.

It was barely daybreak when Joanna and I got to the tomb and saw that the stone which Joseph had used for a door, to protect the body from wild animals, that stone had been rolled aside and a weird light was coming from within the cave. Someone was inside with a candle or lantern! It must be grave robbers. But, there was nothing in the tomb to rob. There was nothing in the tomb but Jesus' bloodied and beaten and dead body. Surely, no one would want to steal his body. In fear and trembling, we approached and looked in. And, much to my horror, the worst had happened. — there had been a robbery! Jesus' body had been stolen!

Then, I saw two beings, angels I assumed, sitting at either end of the slab. The source of the light was coming from their brilliance. We both fell to our knees, for we were in great fear. One of the beings spoke, "Do not be afraid. Why seek the living among the dead? He is not here. He has risen. Go and tell the others."

Neither Joanna nor I understood what we were seeing or what we were hearing. But we knew the others must be told at once. Joanna ran to tell Mary, and I went to find the disciples. The men were holed-up in the room where they had shared their last meal together. You see, they feared that they would be arrested and, maybe even killed, since they had been Jesus' supporters.

At first, I couldn't get them to open the door. Finally, I convinced them who I was and that I was alone. Once inside the room, I related the events of the past hour. Most of them felt that my words were just 'idle tales.' A couple of them smiled, patted me on the hand, and said, "Sure, Mary, Sure." But, as a result of my witness, Peter and John bolted out of the room, down the stairs, and through the streets, hurrying to see for themselves. I ran after them, but could not catch up.

I came to the garden alone, while the dew was still on the roses. I didn't see the men, they were nowhere in sight. I don't know where they had gone. But, there I was all alone. Everything was still and quiet. I stood there in that eerie, early morning light. None of this seemed real. Maybe the men were right. Maybe all this was "idle tales of an hysterical woman." Maybe, I had made everything up. Maybe, it was all in my head. I had to make sure.

So, I looked again in the tomb. The slab was still bare, but the angels and the brilliant light were gone. The tomb was, indeed, *empty*.

Suddenly, I was overcome with exhaustion. I was exhausted from all the running I had been doing. I was exhausted from all I had seen and heard. I was exhausted from the confusion I was experiencing. "Who would have taken his body?" "Why would anyone have taken his body?" And, I was exhausted from the profound grief of losing the one person most dear to me. All my dreams of the last three years were as empty as that tomb. All the excitement about bringing God's kingdom to earth — dead! And now, someone had even desecrated our Lord's tomb.

I was no longer able to stand, and so I eased down on a bench in the garden and cried. Not the loud wailing of formal grief, but the soft tears that wash over the body in waves. The gardener approached and asked why I was crying. I resented his intrusion upon my grief, and I blurted out, "Somebody has taken my Master's body and I don't know where they have laid him. Do you know where they've taken him?"

I had not raised my head as I spoke. My eyes were still focused on the ground when the gardener softly said, "Mary." I couldn't believe my ears. No one on earth said my name quite like he did. I recognized that voice. That was my Master's voice. I looked up and looked full in the face of my Lord! "Rabbani!" I cried. "Rabbani, you are alive!" I fell to my knees and reached to kiss his feet.

"Don't touch me," he said. "I have not yet ascended unto my Father. Go and tell my disciples (and Peter) that I ascend unto my Father and your Father, to my God and to your God."

At first, I wondered why Jesus didn't simply instruct me to go and tell the disciples. Why had he deliberately included Peter's name? Peter was the head disciple. But, as soon as I had that thought, I understood.

Peter had messed up so badly. He was constantly misunderstanding the meaning of the parables. He totally misunderstood Jesus' message of peace, evidenced by cutting off one of the soldier's ears in the garden. He had denied our Lord three times to the young servant girl in the courtyard. And, then, didn't even show up at the crucifixion.

Peter had messed up big time. And Jesus, knowing human nature as he does, knew that Peter would not feel himself worthy to be considered part of the group any longer. So, Jesus (even now at this tender moment) in love and compassion, he went out of his way to let Peter know that all had been forgiven.

Oh, I would have stayed in the garden with him, but he bade me go. "Mary, I send you to go and tell others of my resurrection and of my love." I did as Jesus instructed — I went and *told*. So, in a way, I became the first apostle, for that is what the word "apostle" means — "one who was sent." Anyway, I went and witnessed to my personal encounter with my risen Lord, witnessing to everyone I met along the way. Later, Jesus, himself, appeared to all the disciples together while they were gathered in that upper room. And, then, over a period of several weeks, he appeared to many people in many different places. During that time, he opened our minds to understand the scriptures far more than we ever had.

Then, the time came for Jesus to depart — to return to heaven, to take his place at the right hand of God. We begged him to stay, but he explained that if he did not go, the comforter (the Holy Spirit) could not come. But we kept insisting, telling him over and over that we would far rather have him with us. But he explained that it would be better for us to have the Spirit with us. The Spirit would not be limited by time or place — but be within us — and not for a while, but forever.

At the end of those forty days physically with us, he led us out of the city over to the Mount of Olives to a small hill and gave us one last command. "You will be my witnesses in Jerusalem, in all Judea and Samaria, and to the ends of the earth." Yes, I thought, I would gladly witness in Jerusalem, in Judea, even in all Samaria. But how could I ever witness to the ends of the earth? He continued his command: "But, first, tarry in the city until you receive the gift of the Spirit and be endued with power from on high."

Then Jesus began to rise. As a group, we watched breathlessly, as he ascended into heaven. We stood there staring into the empty heavens until two angels appeared and 'dismissed' us.

"What do we do now?" someone asked. Well, Jesus had said for us to remain in the city, so we went back to that upper room where he had shared his last supper with his disciples. The room was uncomfortably crowded because our number had now grown to one hundred twenty people! And we waited. All day — we waited. We saturated ourselves in prayer, and we waited. We waited for the 'gift of the Spirit', whatever that was. For ten long days, we waited and prayed — and prayed and waited.

And, then it happened! The gift of the Holy Spirit was given, in wind, flame, and power. I raised my head and looked around. Each person's face was aglow. And, it looked almost as if 'tongues of fire' rested on each head.

And, then, I felt the presence of the comforter within me. And, I saw Peter (this same Peter who had messed up so badly, who had hidden from the soldiers) — open the door and walk out of hiding and onto the landing and preach to a large crowd who had gathered when they heard the noise of the great wind. And he preached so effectively (remember, this was his first sermon) he preached so effectively that three thousand people were saved that day!

Seeing that miracle, I realized that, with the power of the Holy Spirit, yes I, too, could witness far beyond anything I had dreamed possible. Maybe, I couldn't preach like Peter, or pray like some of the others; but I could show the love of Jesus. I could let them know that Jesus is the "balm of Gilead" spoken of by Jeremiah [13]; that Jesus is the "balm of Gilead" that makes the wounded whole, the "balm of Gilead" that heals the sin-sick soul." I could tell and show the love of Jesus. And, that is what I committed my life to.

And, I understand that the followers of Jesus Christ, down through the centuries, have continued to, not only preach about the love of Jesus — but show that love through bringing hospitals, orphanages, food relief, speaking out for the poor and the downtrodden, and so much more to people everywhere.

13 Jeremiah 8:22 (NRSV)

A while back, I came across a very old hymns which sums up my charge, my commitment. Let me share with you some of the words from that hymn:

Four gospels were written of Jesus, your Lord,
that others his goodness might view;
But many (who miss his written word)
are reading the life you unfold —
the gospel — according to you
of all that you say and you do
Wherever you go, let your life truly show —
the gospel according to you.[14]

Dear friends, this is my prayer for you, that wherever you go, may your life truly show the gospel according to you. Thank you....

14 *The Gospel According to You*, W. C. Poole, copyright 1931 by George W. Cooke — now in the public domain.

SUSANNA WESLEY

Character: *Susanna Wesley — Mother John and Charles Wesley*

Caption: *The "Dr. Spock" Of The Eighteenth Century*

Publicity Blurb: *"Can you imagine giving birth to nineteen children and the grief of losing nine of them in infancy, yet having to continue to maintain the parsonage with a spouse who is away much of the time?"*

Scripture: *Proverbs 22:6*

Hymns: *"A Charge To Keep I Have" by Charles Wesley; "Take Time To Be Holy"*

Scripture Study Prep: *none*

Length of Performance: *word count 3,010*

Dress: *long black skirt; plain white, long sleeve blouse, long white 'half'-apron (no bib), 'Mob' cap with single ribbon.*

Shoes: *unattractive black low heeled shoes with thin, black socks — no black hose*

Accessories: *plain, silver wedding band, no earrings.*

Props: *"old-timey" family Bible which can contain printed "letter" of Susanna's*

Make-up: *very little*

Suggested Season to Perform: *mother-daughter banquet*

Susanna Wesley

The Doctor Spock Of The Eighteenth Century

Hello, my name is Susanna Wesley, mother of John and Charles Wesley and their eight siblings. As you know, John was the founder of the Methodist Movement, and eventually, of the United Methodist Church, though my son never intended to start a new church, only to revive the old, stale, stagnant Church of England.

Before I go any further, let me tell you a little about myself. I was born in London in 1669, the daughter of a minister of the gospel in the dissenter, or non-conformist movement and granddaughter of a successful, wealthy doctor.

I was married on November 11, 1688, to a minister also of the dissenter movement. Most marriages in my day were in the months of November, December, or January because that was when farm duties were the lightest. I was married in my father's parsonage. Well, really it was our own home. Dissenter ministers did not enjoy the luxury of a parsonage provided by the church. Even my wedding was a political statement by my non-conformist father. The bishop of London from the Church of England had demanded that all weddings must take place in the church.

My dowry consisted of linens, household items, and some money from my father. My friends gave us staple goods similar to the later custom of "pounding" and for the same reason that "pounding the minister" later became the custom in the colonies. As dissenters, the ministers were not paid by the government as the priests in the Church of England were, just as the ministers in the colonies were not funded by your government.

Samuel gave me a plain silver wedding band which I was proud to wear. But, somehow, it didn't seem right that he didn't wear a ring also to show his commitment.

My married life was a hard one. Not without its good moments, but it was hard. Money was always in short supply. And, I was pregnant most of the time. Actually, I gave birth to nineteen children. Sadly, nine died in infancy. I, myself, came from a large family. I was the youngest of 25 children! My husband was certainly a man of God, but he wasn't much of a family man. He left me alone with the children many, many times. But, through it all, God and I persevered.

Early in the Methodist movement, John asked me several times to write down my methods of child rearing. After rearing ten children, I certainly had methods for doing so, but I didn't write anything down. You know how children are. They don't really mean for you to do something like that. It's just a way of complimenting you. But he kept asking. John said, "Mother, please write down your methods, for I have group of ladies called Methodists who could benefit from your methods." I told him all that was needed was a Bible and prayer. But John wanted something more concrete — more practical. And so, finally I wrote down my methods.

You see, I have always believed that anything worth doing, is worth doing well, and to do anything well requires a plan — a method. By the way, you know where the name "Methodist" comes from, don't you? The term began when John and Charles were away at University, at Christ College, Oxford. They had formed what they called the "Holy Club." The group would pray and study the scriptures — and then go out into the streets and prisons, doing what good they could. And my boys had learned well from me that anything worth doing is worth doing well and that to do something well requires a plan — a method.

And so, they developed a method for their ministries. On Mondays, they visited the prisons; on Tuesdays, they visited the hospital; on Wednesdays, they dispensed food and what medicines they could obtain to the homeless on the streets; and so on. Some of their fellow seminary students made fun of them and claimed they were so "methodical" that they had a method for doing everything — that they were just a bunch of "method-ists". And so, the name stuck.

Knowing that I was to speak to you today, I looked through my papers and found my rough draft of that letter I sent to John. Now I realize that many of you have already reared your children. And many of my methods, my rules would not fit you in your present day. But I believe the core of my instruction hasn't changed and that there is, probably, still a group of ladies called Methodists, and some who are not Methodists who could benefit from my methods. So, please, accept these words in the spirit they are offered.

Now, I wrote my methods down a very long time ago. The letter was dated July 24, 1732, so please forgive me if I read from a copy of that letter.[15]

"*First of all, it must be understood that the rearing and instruction of the children is the responsibility of both mother and father. And there must be an agreement between the two on the methods used, so that the child is not pulled this way or that.*" Now, I understand that in your day, unfortunately, often there is not both a mother and a father in the home. Oh my, what a difficult task for one to undertake alone. But if it *is* a single parent, then it is paramount that whoever is assisting, be it a relative or even a servant, in the rearing of the children, must be in one accord with the parent.

"*Second, it must be understood that the instruction of children is a sacred obligation and cannot be carried out successfully without God's help, for the primary duty of a parent is to save their child's soul.*

"*Third, a mother must find a way to care for herself in the midst of all that is going on around her, be it reading or writing, a time of reflection or simply a solitary walk in the woods.*" Now, I was incredibly busy, but I found a way. And you know those times when you feel that you will just explode if you can't have just a few moments without your children pulling on you? Well, I developed a method for that, too. I would lift my long white apron, like this one which I wore daily. I would lift this apron up over my head. When that apron was up, the children knew that Mother was not home. And they also understood that blood must be flowing before they dare interrupt.

And "*fourth, the importance of a regular schedule cannot be too much emphasized. The children were always put into a regular method of living, in such things as they were capable of; as in dressing and undressing, changing their bed sheets, carrying out their chores, getting*

15 Rebecca Lamar Harman, *Susanna: Mother of the Wesleys* (Nashville, TN: Abingdon Press, 1968).

up and going to bed and taking their meals at pre-set times. A child needs that structure in their life, as well as the structure and discipline of loving parents.

"From the beginning, the children were put into their cradle awake and rocked to sleep, so that they understood that when rocked, they were to sleep.

"When turned a year old, they were taught to fear the rod and to cry only softly, by which means they escaped abundance of correction which they might otherwise have had, and that most odious noise of the crying of children was rarely heard in the house, but the family usually lived in such quietness as if there had been not a child among them.

"As soon as they could take solid food, they were brought to the children's table which sat by ours. They were confined to three meals a day. And they were taught to eat whatever was set before them. So constantly were they used to eating and drinking what was given them, that when any of them was ill, there was no difficulty in making them take the most unpleasant medicine. And, of course, eating and drinking between meals was never allowed.

"At six o'clock in the evening, as soon as prayers were over, they had their supper. At seven o'clock, they were bathed; and beginning with the youngest, dressed and put to bed, hopefully by eight o'clock, at which time they were left in their rooms awake, for there was no such thing allowed in our house as sitting by a child till he fell asleep.

"In order to form the minds of children, the first thing to be done is to conquer their will and bring them to an obedient temper. To inform the understanding is a work of time, and must, with children, proceed by slow degrees, as they are able to bear it. But the subjecting the will is a thing which must be done at once, and the sooner the better, for by neglecting timely correction they will contract a stubbornness and obstinacy which is hardly ever conquered."

I know this sounds harsh, but I cannot yet dismiss this subject. There are those parents whom the world deems kind and indulgent, whom I call *cruel* parents, who permit their children to get habits which they know must be afterward broken, and often by very strenuous means or leave the child to his own waywardness. Now understand this: As self-will is the root of all sin and misery, the parent has a God-given responsibility to do what is necessary to ensure the salvation of their child's soul.

"Our children were taught the Lord's Prayer almost before they could talk. And they were made to say it upon rising each morning and, of course, at bedtime. As they grew bigger, short prayers for their parents, some short printed prayers, a short catechism, and some short portion of scripture were added to the evening prayer. They were very early made to distinguish the sabbath from other days and were as soon taught to be still at family prayers.

"They were quickly made to understand that they might have nothing they cried and shouted for. They were not allowed to ask, even from one of the servants, for anything without saying, 'Pray, please, may I have such a thing?' Taking the Lord's name in vain, cursing and swearing, profanity, obscenity, rude ill-bred names — were never heard among them.

"The schooling of the children was in the home, to which I devoted six hours each day." It is almost incredible what may be taught a child in a quarter of a year by a vigorous application. "It was the practice in my home to teach each child his letters on the day of his fifth birthday. Then, beginning at the first chapter of Genesis, the child was made to spell the first verse, read it over and over until done without hesitation, and so on with the next verse. Ten verses constituted the lesson." All my children were fine readers and correct spellers.

"Though home-schooled, my husband and I endeavored to provide the broadest of opportunities. For our children the course of study consisted of Latin, Greek, French, logic, metaphysics, literature, ciphering, the scriptures, and what scientific knowledge we could impart. I taught French. Samuel conducted the classes in Latin and Greek." My daughter Hetty, could read Greek at the age of eight and in later life was in the inner circle of literary figures who frequented the home of Dr. Samuel Johnson.

Now, this point was extremely important to me, even though it was almost three hundred years ago. And so I wrote: "I taught my daughters the domestic skills which were expected and required of them; such as cooking and sewing, doing the laundry, planting a kitchen garden, canning and preserving. But those domestic skills were not taught until the girls had mastered all the academic studies that were taught the boys.

"Lessons did not consist only of religious and educational instruction. And so, it was important to include a list of family activities which were

138

both recreational and instructional and which strengthened the family bond."

While I cared nothing for such worldly amusements as ballroom dancing, I did have a dance master come to the house to give lessons. I also played cards (not those nasty gambling cards with pictures of kings and queens on them — but children's cards). But — yes, I played cards and other games with the children frequently. With ten children, it was easy to teach many of the classics by way of small dramas, and my children grew adept at taking some of the driest prose and transforming it into interesting dramatic presentations. There was little money for store-bought toys, but the house was filled with those made by our own hands. The children also followed a regimen of outdoor exercise and wholesome fun.

I continued to write: *"It was also important to make each child feel as an individual, as special, and not simply one of a brood. To this end, I devoted a special time of two hours each week to spend alone with each child, where we related as mother and child, as friends, and not as school instructor or disciplinarian.* (Ten children — two hours each week — You do the math!) John's time was on Thursday evenings and I was blessed to read, years later, that he still recalled those times together fondly.

Following the big fire in which John was so miraculously rescued, "as a brand plucked from the fire" the children were, of necessity, parceled out to neighbors until the parsonage could be rebuilt. When we were all together again under one roof, I was appalled at what had transpired during those few months in the absence of my discipline and schedule. Therefore, certain by-laws were written down and observed thereafter. Here is a list of those by-laws:

1) "It had been observed that cowardice and fear of punishment often leads children into lying until they get a custom of it which they cannot leave. To prevent this, a law was made that whoever was charged with the fault of which they were guilty, if they would confess it promptly and promise to amend their ways, (that is, to never do it again),

they should not be beaten. This rule prevented a great deal of lying.

2) "That no sinful action, as lying, pilfering at church or on the Lord's Day, disobedience, quarreling, and the like, should never go unpunished.

3) "That no child should ever be scolded or beat twice for the same offense, and that if they amended their ways, that mistake or sin, should never be brought up again.

4) "That every single act of obedience, especially when it crossed upon their own inclinations, should be always commended, and frequently rewarded according to the merits of the case.

5) "That if ever any child perform an act of obedience, or do anything with an intention to please, though the performance was not well, the action should be kindly accepted, and the child, with sweetness, directed how to do better in the future.

6) "That the rights of property were invariably preserved. No child was allowed to invade the property of another, even in the smallest matter. That one child might not take from the owner something without (much less against) the owner's consent. This rule can never be too much inculcated on the minds of children.

7) "That promises must be strictly observed; and a gift once bestowed, cannot be taken back."

And finally,

8) "That parents should at all times, when possible, abide by the same by-laws."

I know my words such as beating a child, or conquering their will, or not allowing a child to cry but softly, may seem cruel to you. But I assure you, no mother ever loved her children more, or worked harder to train up her children in the ways they should go. I *committed my ways unto the Lord,* and I believe, *he directed my path.*

For although my ways seem harsh to you, seem designed to break the spirit of my children, nothing could have been further from the truth. I loved my daughters very much and was proud of them. In an age when little could be accomplished by women, (except to marry well), my daughters experienced a certain amount of success. Emily became a governess; first to a private family, then in a boarding school, and finally (with some help from her brother John) set up her own school. Hetty (the little girl who could read Greek at the age of eight), was a published poet and wrote for a literary magazine.

My son, Samuel Junior, enjoyed a good, strong ministry as a priest in the Church of England. All three of my sons were ordained as priests in the Church of England. Charles, who was also a poet, ended up writing over 6,000 hymns during his lifetime.

And John. What can I say about John? He had difficulty at first "finding himself", or more properly, "finding God's unique will" for his life. But after returning to England from a very unsuccessful mission trip to your colony of Georgia, he attended a service on Aldersgate Street and had, what he described later, a heartwarming experience. And after that "spiritual rebirth," he was able to lead a great revival in England which some historians credit with sparing England the kind of bloody revolution which plagued France at that time.

Oh, everything did not turn out perfectly with my children. Most of my daughters did not marry well. And, neither did my son John! Unfortunately, his marriage was a dismal mistake. All I can say is that with God' s help, I did all that I could do. And, in the end, that is all any mother can do.

Thank you, again, for allowing me to come and share my thoughts with you.

MRS. SUSANNA WESLEY

Character: *Mrs. Susanna Wesley — Mother of John and Charles Wesley*

Caption: *The "Mother Of Methodism"*

Publicity Blurb: *"Can you imagine my pride as I see the lasting, world-wide influence of my sons, John and Charles, and knowing that God allowed me to train them up in the way they should go?"*

Scripture: *Mark 12:29-31*

Hymns: *"Love Divine, All Loves Excelling" by Charles Wesley*

Scripture Study Prep: *none*

Length of Performance: *word count 3,147*

Dress: *long black skirt; fancy long sleeve blouse; "pinner" cap with lace*

Shoes: *unattractive black low-heeled shoes with thin, black socks — no black hose*

Accessories: *no jewelry except plain silver wedding band and broach at neck*

Props: *hand-outs of John Wesley quotes*

Make-up: *very plain*

Suggested Season to Perform: *Heritage Sunday; Aldersgate Sunday*

Mrs. Samuel Wesley (Susanna)

MOTHER Of Methodism
Mother Of John And Charles Wesley

Hello. My name is Mrs. Samuel Wesley, better known to you as Susanna. Thank you for inviting me here. Of course, to you I am known as the mother of John and Charles Wesley. But I feel I must remind you that I am also the mother of Samuel Junior and seven girls. In all, I gave birth to nineteen children, only ten of whom survived. And I'm sure you all consider my son John as the founder, or father, of Methodism. But perhaps, I am the mother of Methodism.

My father was a non–conformist, or dissenter minister. At this time in history, the established church, the Church of England, was somewhat corrupt, but more importantly, it was stale — stagnant. It had, as the apostle Paul told young Timothy, it "had a form of godliness — but had denied the power thereof." My father, and some of the others, perhaps influenced by the Pietist movement, felt that they could no longer "conform" to the rules and regulations and politics of the church — but must, instead, follow the dictates of their hearts.

Because the dissenter movement was so "politically incorrect" in my day, the usual seminaries were closed to the young men of that persuasion. (Talk about non-open doors.) My father had some independent monies, (My grandfather was an important medical doctor in London.) And so, my father owned a large home in downtown London. When he learned that the seminaries had closed their doors to these young men, he opened the doors of his house and his very large library to these young, dissenter seminarians. And, he went a step further. He would invite some of his friends, fellow "dissenter" ministers, to come over for a time of open discussion, to which he invited the young men to participate. I would love sitting on the staircase outside the library, listening to their discussions. Because my father believed strongly that our God created *all that is*, the discussions were not limited to doctrinal and theological discussion. Literally anything under heaven was open for discussion. And so, I began my life with an *open mind* and *open doors* and an *open heart*.

One of the young men who came to our home was Samuel Wesley, whose father was also a "dissenter" minister. As soon as I was old enough, we were married. Our first appointment was to a very small parish with a very small congregation and an equally small salary. But we were young and in love. Our time there was not pleasant. One of the reasons was that though my husband had many wonderful qualities, unfortunately, tact was not one of them. Another reason: I became pregnant very early in our marriage and the pregnancy was very difficult — requiring me to spend much of my time in bed. The delivery was also difficult and it was necessary to stay in bed for a few additional weeks. Rather than gaining the sympathy of the women of the church, they saw me as a young, spoiled rich girl who thought my pregnancy gave me an excuse to be lazy. I think my husband's attitude was much to blame for the way they felt about me.

Like I said, my husband was blessed with an opinion on everything, and unfortunately, he was vocal on most of them, even to our parishioners. He saw great problems with the Church of England, as did I. Unfortunately, was he not only *vocal* in his opposition, but put those objections into print in the form of a stream of letters to the editor of our London newspaper.

One day he was approached by a delegation from the Church of England, who convinced him to join them, persuading him that he could be more effective in bringing about change from *within* the system. Unfortunately, he agreed without discussing the matter with me. I was very skeptical of his decision. But of course, I had no voice in his decision. I was only his wife.

But my intuition proved true. Our first appointment in the Church of England was to the parish at Epworth, in the north part of the country. Now I know that we are not supposed to feel this way, but we all know that there is one particular appointment that really *is* the worst in the district or conference or whatever geographic area there is. Epworth was that appointment. The land was hard and rough — as were the people. And, they were uneducated. Now, while I personally enjoy the company of more learned people, I do not look down on the less fortunate. I had worked with the uneducated of London and would have gladly done the same at Epworth. But these people were different. They were uneducated and proud of it.

Now, it was into this culture that the Church of England chose to send my erudite, opinionated, tact-less husband. My husband was embroiled in a very heated argument even before we got our wagon unloaded. I could see from this beginning that this was going to be another unpleasant appointment. But there is one good thing about the itinerant system. No appointment lasts forever. Well, guess what, Epworth did! My husband was never appointed anywhere else.

Life was hard. Money was in short supply. Church attendance was tiny. My husband was not accepted by the community. And, if the truth be known, he was not accepted by many members of our own congregation. Again, my husband's lack of tact played a major role. My husband had an interesting way of escaping much of our unpleasantness. He would 'volunteer' to attend constant seminars and conferences and convocations. He was always welcomed as a leader to these events because he represented the token opposition, making the church seem all the more open. There were two things wrong with this picture. Not only did that leave me home alone to raise my ten children, but the most unfortunate aspect of all this was that there was no *per diem*, no reimbursement of finances. And, my financial plight was so bad that, on more than one occasion, I found it necessary to contact the bishop to obtain food for my children.

Like I said, when thing got heated — my husband looked for some place to go. Luck was on his side this one time. Let me tell you about it. My husband had, yet again, angered many of the townspeople. He volunteered (No wait — this time he was *asked*) to serve as a delegate to a very prestigious convocation on the mainland that would last four months. For this convocation, he was given a very small stipend — only enough to cover his travel, room and board.

The problem was that to be gone from his parish for that length of time required him to hire an interim pastor, which he would have to pay out of his meager salary. As I have said, money was scarce. And so, my husband searched for the cheapest replacement he could find.

When the man arrived, he looked all right enough. But when I heard him preach for the first time, I understood why he came so cheap. I'm sure the man knew his scripture and, probably, all the correct doctrinal points, but the man couldn't preach! My ten children and I sat stoically in the pew, but I knew many of our parishioners would not abide such preaching. I successfully avoided any comments to any of the church people on the way out. I (and my ten children) returned that evening for the service of Evensong. Evensong has always been my favorite service. It is set, as the name implies, at twilight or at the beginning of the evening. In the high-steeple churches, the service was a highly, formal, ritualized choral service. But, here in a small rural parish, the service consisted mainly of scripture, prayers from the *Common Book of Prayers*, a hymn or two, and a short homily. I don't know how he did it but this man's Evensong was as lack-luster as the morning service. But, being the pastor's wife, I had no choice but to attend all services. I believed firmly that one must attend to all the ordinances of God, the first being the public attendance of worship.

I, then, was outraged when the interim announced, after only two of the evening services, that Evensong would be canceled. He stated his reason as lack of attendance. This really did anger me because my husband was paying him to conduct those services. It also angered me because, as I had mentioned, it was my favorite service. I also felt it was the most important service for my children, because in this service one was more able to get in touch with one's feelings, with one's heart.

On the way home from services, my anger grew with each step I took. When we arrived at the parsonage, I instructed the children to go upstairs and change out of their Sunday clothes and to not disturb me. I went to my room, sat in my rocking chair and began to pray. I knew I had to rid my heart of all this anger, this bitterness. I rocked and prayed, prayed and rocked, until I "prayed through." (Are you familiar with this phrase?) But I was not finished. Once the bitterness was gone — I needed to pray for guidance. What now? How do I handle this situation? Again, I "prayed through" until I had a peace and a direction. When time for the Evensong service grew near, I instructed my children to put their Sunday clothes back on and join me in the parlor. There, we held our own private Evensong.

I met a parishioner at the market a few days after the first canceled service. And though I tried not to bad-mouth this interim, she pushed me to know my reaction to the cancellation of that service. To which I replied that I had continued to hold that service, only in the privacy of my own home. I explained to her that, at the appropriate time, we assembled in the front room, Charles played the piano, we all sang, we all prayed, we all listened to the scripture being read, and I read a short portion of one of my husband's sermons. My friend asked if she and her family could join us the following Sunday evening. Because I have always believed that my home should be open to anyone seeking spiritual nourishment and because I believe in *open doors*, (remembering the closed doors of years ago) I agreed.

When that Sunday evening arrived, I was surprised that she had brought several more families with her. Each Sunday evening the crowd grew until it was too large for our small house. Whereupon, I opened the windows and invited friends to stand outside, trampling down my flower bed. I grew uncomfortable simply reading my husband's words and, because of my Pietist tradition, felt more comfortable in sharing my own thoughts. And because the crowd had grown so large, I felt it more practical to divide the group up into small groups where they could discuss, speak from their heart, what had been lifted up from scripture and my words.

In just a few short weeks, I was attracting more people to my Sunday evening service than the interim pastor was to his Sunday morning service. This was embarrassing to the new man, and so he wrote a letter to my husband claiming that I was acting in a way unbecoming to a pastor's wife. My husband wrote me a very short letter, saying "Stop!" I wrote back to my sometime clueless husband that I would be glad to stop the services if he was sure that that was what God wanted me to do. His return letter was also very short. It simply said, "Continue as God leads you."

I know this was a very unusual practice in my day — a woman preaching to a group of men — but perhaps my son Jacky saw the value of *open hearts, open minds, open doors*. Maybe, he also saw the value of *small groups*. And, maybe, seeing me in this leadership role under extraordinary circumstances, allowed my son to actually ordain a couple of women in what he termed extraordinary appointments.

I was so pleased to find out that when my sons, Charles and John, went off to university at Christ Church, Oxford, they formed what they called the Holy Club to spend time in prayer and Bible study. I was even more pleased when I learned that they had understood what I had tried to instill in them, that *one cannot separate personal piety from social action*. As John once said, *"The gospel of Christ knows no religion but social; no holiness but social holiness."* It is my understanding that they had developed a method for this social action, of *doing good*. You see, it is not enough to simply *do no harm*. One must also *actively do good* — as John's motto would later state.

And so, on Mondays they visited the hospital; on Tuesdays they visited the prisons; on Wednesdays they dispensed medicine on the streets to the poor.

I understand that some of their college friends made fun of them, claiming that they had a method of doing everything — that they were just a group of "Method-ist". And, of course, the name stuck. And, I understand that this same system of *Methods* is still alive and well within the church that bears that name today. Methods are important. I have always believed that anything worth doing is worth doing well. And I have always believed that to do anything well, one must have a method. And so, I was pleased that John had developed such a methodology.

I remember one time, early in the Methodist movement, that John asked me to write down my methods of child rearing. As I mentioned, I was blessed with the God-given task of raising ten children. I took this mission very seriously, and so, I had a very structured method of child-rearing. I was flattered that he asked me to share my methods, but I didn't comply. The next time he was home, he asked again saying, "Please write down your methods, for I have a group of ladies, called 'Methodist', who would greatly benefit from your wisdom." And, so, I did. Imagine my surprise to learn that my list of methods has survived and is included in a book available in bookstores.[16]

And so, you see, my attention (some might say my obsession) to methods led my son to grow up interpreting the world and his faith through methods he developed. One of those methods involved learning to interpret God's will in the modern world. It had four components and a fancy name, "quadrilateral". It involved basing one's understanding on scripture, tradition, reason, and experience. These four being equal, but one — scripture — being a little bit more "equal" than the others.

SCRIPTURE

Well, before you can base your understanding on scripture, you must know that scripture. From a very early age, I instilled in each of my children the totality of the scripture. And, my son, Jacky, learned his scripture quite well. At one time, he was referred to as "The Man of One Book" — that book being the Holy Bible — though his saddlebags were loaded down with books of all categories, even a tract on how to cure baldness.

SCRIPTURE — TRADITION

My husband, being a priest in the Church of England, as were all three of our sons, was able to cover the tradition part of this formula quite well. He loved history, ritual, and ceremonies. He knew the scriptures well and was careful to interpret the scripture as it had traditionally been interpreted down through the centuries. So, my husband contributed much to the tradition.

SCRIPTURE — TRADITION — REASON

My son grew up during the time the history books refer to as the *Age of Reason*, and reason fit my son's mind and his personality quite well. Because he knew the scriptures in their entirety, he knew that there were some seeming contradictions. John believed that it was at this time reason could be used to help

16 Susanna: Mother of the Wesleys, by Rebecca Lamar Harman, Abingdon Press, Nashville 1968

clarify the meaning, the balance; how tradition had interpreted the passages; what made sense in the world today. You see, he knew that when Jesus quoted Moses on the great commandment, Jesus added *"You shall love the Lord your God with your heart and soul, mind, and strength."* God gave us a mind — let's use it. And he remembered also the words of Isaiah, *"Come, let us reason together."*

SCRIPTURE — TRADITION — REASON — EXPERIENCE

And finally, John listed experience. And I understand that different people understand that word to mean different things. But for me, especially with my Pietist influence, (and I believe for my son) Experience means my own personal experience, what works in the heart for me — what allows my heart to be touched — to be *strangely warmed.*

You see, the *heart* is at the core of it all, for out of the heart does love flow. My son summed up the gospel by saying, *"Love God — Love Others."* It was this love of others which led my son to say: *"If we cannot all think alike — can we not all love alike?"*

Now, my son well knew that we do *not* all think alike. And, he firmly believed that some ways of thinking were far better than others. And, he was like his father in having an opinion on most things. But where he differed from his father was that John had a little bit of humility. Oh, I know. People don't usually list humility as one of his traits. But, his love of others allowed him to say, on more than one occasion, *"What is as clear for me as the sun at noonday, is not so clear to everyone."*

But he made this distinction. He said, *that Jesus Christ is the Son of God, that he died for our sins and was raised from the dead and reigns in heaven to make intercession for us* — this belief is bedrock, not open for discussion, not open for various opinions. But he went on to say: *"All other belief — all other — is opinion; and for opinion's sake let us not argue. If your heart is right, give me your hand. Come, let us worship together."*

Thank you for letting me share my recollections of the beginnings of the people called *Methodists.*

Wesley's structure for the Christian pilgrimage of discipleship:

(1) Do no harm

(2) Do good

(3) Attend upon all the ordinances of God: public worship, Bible study, regularly receiving the Lord's Supper, family and private prayer, and fasting.

Wesley's Words Of Wisdom

❖ If we cannot all think alike, can we not all love alike?

❖ The gospel of Christ knows no religion but social; no holiness but social holiness.

❖ You cannot separate personal piety from social action.

❖ What is as clear for me as the sun at noonday is not so clear to everyone.

❖ <u>Earn</u> all the money you can; so that you may <u>save</u> all the money you can; in order that you may <u>give</u> all the money you can!

❖ For opinions' sake, let us not argue. If your heart is right, give me your hand. Come, let us worship together.

Wesley's Motto
Do all the good you can,
By all the means you can,
In all the ways you can,
In all the places you can,
At all the times you can,
To all the people you can,
As long as ever you can.

Wesley's Quadrilateral
1) Scripture
2) Tradition
3) Reason
4) Experience

A Prayer Of Susanna Wesley

You, O Lord, have called us to watch and pray. Therefore, whatever may be the sin against which we pray, make us careful to watch against it, and so have reason to expect that our prayers will be answered. In order to perform this duty aright, grant us grace to preserve a sober, equal temper, and sincerity to pray for your assistance. Amen.

— from *The United Methodist Book of Worship*

KATIE VON BORA LUTHER

Character: *Katharina von Bora Luther, wife of Martin Luther (1499-1552)*

Caption: *The Morning Star of Wittenberg*

Publicity Blurb: *"Can you imagine what it is like to manage a forty- room home, rear six children, oversee a cattle breeding enterprise and a brewery, farm many acres, and be the "pastor's wife" to the most famous pastor in the world?"*

Scripture read: *Ephesians 2: 5–9; 5: 22, 25, 21*

Hymns: *"A Mighty Fortress Is Our God" "Amazing Grace"*

Length of Performance: *word count 4,045, approximately 32 minutes*

Dress: *floor-length black or muted skirt with wide colored bands. Blouse with wide square, low neck opening and full, billowing long sleeves, fastened tightly at the wrists. A short cape might be added or a colorful sleeve-less over-garment, freely flowing to the floor.*

Hair: *black hood over white cap with roped coil underneath to heighten the hood. A black veil attached to the back of the hood. The hood is worn far back on the head, exposing the hair, which is parted in the middle.*

(Portrait available online)

Shoes: *broad, flat, square-toed, almost sandal like, fastened with a strap across the instep.*

Accessories: *plain wedding band, cameo broche at collar.*

Props: *old, worn Bible.*

Make-up: *none, especially no lipstick*

Suggested Season to Perform: *around Reformation Sunday, October 31*

Kartharina von Bora Luther

The Morning Star Of Wittenberg

Hello, thank you for inviting me here today to share my story with you. My name is Katharina von Bora Luther, but my friends call me Katie. Oh, where do I start my story? Well, I guess the beginning is a good place to start.

I was born in the year 1499 in the country of Germany. My father was of the landed gentry. Unfortunately, by the time I came along, most of the land had been sold off and while we were not in poverty, we had a very modest existence. We still retained the title of nobility, but had very little money.

I was one of five children; three brothers and a sister. Though there was little money, I had a happy early childhood. But, unfortunately, my mother died when I was only five years old. Can you imagine how difficult that is for a child of five? But I did have my father and siblings.

I guess my life would have been all right except for what happened next. My father remarried in a very short time so now, at the age of five, I had to get over the loss of my mother and the introduction of a new stepmother. But then, things got even worse. My father shipped both my sister and me off to a convent, which was something like a boarding school, possibly because both my father's sister and my mother's sister were nuns.

Still, now I had to deal with the loss of my mother, the loss of my father and brothers, and even the loss of my home. Life in the convent was not terrible and, though I didn't realize it at the time, this was a common practice for many families of less than affluent means. I truly felt adrift in this world. I don't know what I would have done if it had not been for my sister.

But then, just as I was settling into the convent I was transferred to another, one of the Cistercian-order. This move definitely had some advantages, for both my father's and my mother's sisters were there. My father's sister, my aunt, was even the Mother Superior.

Growing up in the convent was not so bad. But, somehow, it was just not my cup of tea. Though the nuns were good to me, they were also very strict and harsh. And the rules — oh, the rules! There was a rule for almost everything. And I don't know why, but I rebelled against all these rules.

When I turned sixteen, I had a great decision to make. My schooling there at the convent had ended and I would have to leave and go out into the world on my own. I was not prepared for this. And I knew I could not count on my father's help. You see, in my day it was very difficult for an unattached woman of modest means to make her living in the world. I made the decision to become a nun myself.

Now, to take a vow at only sixteen years old might seem like such a big step. But for me it really wasn't such a big step. While I had not felt a strong religious calling to go into the ministry as a nun, the fact was that the church, the convent, would provide me with food to eat, a roof over my head, and a certain standing in the community.

And the vow — a vow of chastity, poverty, obedience, and prayer — (basically the same vow as a monk) did not seem like such a big deal. I had known poverty from an early age. Well, not exactly poverty, but a very austere life. Prayer had been a part of my everyday life from my birth. Chastity was also not a problem for me. Remember, I had grown up in the convent and there were no boys there past the age of ten. I had never had a boyfriend. I had never even really had any boys who were my friends. And, obedience, like I said, I had been raised in the convent under incredible obedience, both to the church and to the nuns. I took the irrevocable vow, knowing that I could never in all my life change those vows or leave the convent.

Well, let me tell you. Once I became a nun, I saw the inner workings of the convent and my eyes were opened. I knew as a child growing up there that there were some abuses. But I just assumed that's the way things were. But now, as a full-fledged nun, I could see the abuses more clearly and I could see the great corruption within the church itself.

I became disturbed. I certainly didn't like what I saw, but I was completely helpless to change anything. All nuns were instructed by our Mother Superior — not my aunt but a different Mother Superior, not only when to pray, but on exactly how to pray and what to pray for. It bothered me greatly that our prayers were to be directed against this monk by the name of Martin Luther and the disturbing movement that he was causing as he spoke out against the corruption and abuses within the church. It bothered me greatly that our prayers were not to be directed against the abuses and corruption itself.

One day, one of the nuns smuggled in a secret pamphlet written by Dr. Luther. I had been familiar with Luther's 95 *Theses* which he had so publicly nailed to the door of Castle Church at the University of Wittenberg. (By the way, the 500th celebration of that day was celebrated on October 31, 2017.) This nailing his 'manifesto' to a church door might seem a strange way for him to make public his protest and call for reform, but this door was something of a public bulletin board in our day, similar to you posting something on your Facebook.

Dr. Luther had been prompted to make this public declaration by the flagrant selling of indulgences by a priest named Johannes Tetzel. Allowed, even encouraged by the pope, these indulgences granted a partial remission of time to be spent in purgatory, the waiting room of sorts in the afterlife before being admitted into heaven. The indulgence was something like a "get out of jail free" card, except that it was a "get out of purgatory" card and it was not free. It was very expensive. This practice resulted in the wealthy being able to *buy* their way into heaven. In his 95 points, he elaborated on many points of corruption, but it really boiled down to three main themes. "First", he wrote, "selling indulgences is wrong because it is done only to raise money to finance the building of the great St. Peter's Basilica; second, the pope has no power, no jurisdiction, over purgatory; and finally, buying gives people a false sense of security and endangers their salvation."

Luther's public proclamation set off what would later be called the Protestant Reformation, the protesting in favor of reform. As this movement grew in strength, Luther was hauled into court before the Diet of Worms in 1521. (Isn't that a weird name? Diet of Worms? But, "Diet" simply meant "Parliament" or "Legislative Body." And "Worms" simply referred to the town in which the court case was heard.)

In this trial, Dr. Luther was threatened with imprisonment or worse if he refused to recant the claims he had made in his infamous *95 Theses*. His reply was (and I have written it down so that I might not misquote), he wrote, **"Unless I am convinced by the testimony of the scriptures or by clear reason (for I do not trust either in the pope or in councils alone, since it is well known that they have often erred and contradicted themselves), I am bound by the scriptures that I have quoted and my conscience is captive to the word of God. I *cannot* and *will not recant* anything, since it is neither safe nor right to go against conscience. *Here I stand. I can do no other.* May God help me."**

Well, as you might imagine, the verdict of that trial went very badly against Dr. Luther. The edict banned his writings and ordered his arrest. Fortunately, he was able to make his escape and was hidden away in a royal castle at Wartburg, where he remained in seclusion for almost a year. But he did not waste that year. Instead, he devoted himself to the translation of the New Testament into German, the common language of the people. You see, before this time, the common translation of the scriptures was written in the Latin vulgate, meaning that only the priests and the very highly educated could read the holy scriptures. This meant that all the common people knew of the scriptures was what was told to them by their priests. You can see what power this gave the church over the people. Dr. Luther did not only translate the scriptures into German, but translated the scriptures from the original Greek *Koine*.

As God would have it, during this time of work as Dr. Luther poured over the scriptures, he came across that beautiful passage in the book of Ephesians, second chapter, where Paul stated that (here, let me read it to you)…

"Even when we were dead in sins, God hath quickened us together with Christ, and hath raised us up *together*, and made us sit *together* in heavenly places in Christ Jesus. For by *grace* are ye saved through faith; and not of yourselves. It is the gift of God, *not of works*, lest any man should boast."[1]

1 Ephesians 2:5-9 (King James Version).

This was an eye opener for Dr. Luther in two ways. He saw, so clearly, that it was not through our good works, not through terrible deprivation like he had endured all those years as a monk, deprivation like fasting to the point of injuring his health, of subjecting his body to almost torture, all trying to gain God's grace. None of that matters, for it was only through the loving grace of God, through the loving gift from God that we receive salvation. And he also saw in this one passage what he would later refer to as the "priesthood of all believers." For in Paul's own words, he claimed that God had raised *us up together* with Christ and made us to sit *together* with Jesus. We were all equal in God's sight. This was a revolutionary thought!

Reading this secret pamphlet, I was more emboldened than ever to do something. I prayed and I felt that God was leading me to leave the convent. Eleven other nuns also felt led to leave. I was able to contact Dr. Luther, who arranged for our escape in the wagon of a herring merchant by the name of Koope, who was the father of one of the nuns. We were smuggled out of the convent in his wagon. Some people said that we were stuffed into the barrels of herrings. But, actually, we were only stuffed down between the barrels.

You may wonder why we had to go to such extraordinary lengths to leave. It was because, at this time, smuggling nuns was a capital offense, punishable by death in all the lands of the Holy Roman Empire. This was serious stuff. This escape occurred on Easter Eve in 1523. Dr. Luther was so moved by our daring escape that, a few months later, he wrote a pamphlet titled "Why Nuns May, with God's Blessing, Leave the Cloisters." I agreed with his words, but it was a great comfort to see a man of his statue and reputation put my thoughts on paper.

So, now, what? As I have said, it was difficult for an un-attached woman to make it in the real world without some man, a father, brother or other male relative to be her "protector." Now Dr. Luther had twelve nuns on his hands. He felt responsible for us. At first, he asked the parents and relatives of us "refugee nuns" to take us again into their homes, but they refused, possibly fearing retribution from the law. So, Dr. Luther set about finding us all husbands.

I appreciated his concern, but this did not set well with me. Within two years, the other women were "married off," most to monks who had followed Dr. Luther and also left the monasteries. But not me. Dr. Luther arranged for me to meet a number of possible suitors, but nothing "clicked." I told a friend that I would have no husband other than Luther's friend Nikolaus Amsdorf or the esteemed Dr. Luther himself.

I didn't see the need to have any husband at all. I was perfectly capable of caring for myself, and my independent nature did not attract suitors. I knew that Dr. Luther appreciated me, my intellect, even my strong spirit. But, he had taken his vow of celibacy, and though he had left the monastery, he wasn't sure he could leave that vow. This was alright with me. I explained, once again, to him that I had no need of a husband.

All my life, I had submitted to another, first to my father and then to the church. But, he reminded me of the culture in which we lived, and how hard it would be for me without the "protection" of a husband. He even had scripture to back him up. He reminded me of the biblical story of Ruth and Boaz and how Boaz had felt obligated to marry the widow of a relative, to become, in the Hebrew, her *Go-El* — her legal protector.

Still, I felt uncomfortable. I knew the passage from the fifth chapter of Ephesians where Paul told the women to be submissive to their husbands. I think every man everywhere knows that scripture. And, I didn't want to have to submit to any man. And, in my day, even the words of the marriage ceremony included the words that I would pledge to love, honor, and *obey* my husband.

But, as Dr. Luther and I studied that scripture together, we came to see that there was more to those words. Let me share those words with you. It does say, **Wives submit yourselves unto your husbands, as unto the Lord.** But it goes on to say, **Husbands, love your wives even as Christ also loved church, and gave himself for it.** And it gets even better. Paul also writes, **Submitting yourselves one to another in the fear of the Lord.**

I realized then, that if a man loved me as much as Christ loved the church, I would have no fear in submitting to that man. Finally, overcoming both our reservations, we were married. And, in the years to come, our pet names for each other were "Sir

Doctor" as I acknowledged my submission to him, and his for me was "My lord Katie" as he accepted my bossy, yet beneficial, ways. Word did reach me that he had confided to a friend that "If I can endure conflict with the devil, sin, and a bad conscience, then I can put up with the irritations of Katie von Bora."

These were turbulent times. The Reformation had caused much unrest which led to the Peasants' Revolt, leading some to plunder and destroy much of the Roman Catholic holdings. Unfortunately, a few of the more zealot adherents to the Reformation actually killed some of the priests. An alliance was formed among some of the Lutheran princes who took a strong stand against both the Holy Roman Empire and against the Peasants' Revolt. Skirmishes and battles broke out from time to time and from locale to locale. Yet, the Reformation breathed a fresh air of freedom among so many of the people. I guess it was like that man, Mr. Dickens, wrote so many centuries later: "It was the best of times, it was the worst of times."

Let's start with the best of times. As a wedding present, one of the Lutheran princes gave us an abandoned Augustinian monastery. The monastery became referred to as the Black Cloister. It was a wonderful gift, made more special because this was where Sir Doctor had resided as a friar while studying at the University of Wittenberg. The building was massive, containing forty rooms and even a brewery! The land also included a large cattle and hog breeding enterprise. A few years later, we were able to purchase some farm land from my brother.

As it turned out, I could produce a very high quality of beer which was in demand in the local pubs. The cattle and other barnyard animals kept us in meat and the milk provided us with cheese. I also proved to have a green thumb. My gardening kept us in vegetables and in grains for bread. All this financial success was necessary, for this Black Cloister monastery had needed to be almost completely renovated. We even rented out many of the rooms to students at the nearby university. All this greatly supplemented my husband's salary as Professor of Theology at the University and pastor of the church.

We needed all the revenue we could generate in order to cover the expenses of the renovations, the serving the many guests who visited on a regular basis, and of rearing our children. I suffered one miscarriage, but was able to give birth to six children. I loved each one dearly. Truly, my children were my pride and joy.

You think of Martin as a great man, and indeed he was. But he was just a man, with his own share of faults and failures. He was given to rather dramatic mood swings. In 1527, when forces came against him from seemingly all sides, it was almost more than he could bear. Then, his dear friend was martyred. He became angry at God, and he did what the apostle Paul warned us all against, he *grew weary in well doing*. The combination of grief, anger, frustration, and high blood pressure created a crisis of faith.

I tried to help, but this was something he had to work out on his own. And, he did. His solution was where he always knew it would be — in the word of God. Martin was drawn to Psalm 46, *God is our refuge and strength, a very present help in trouble*. Martin lived with these words day in and day out. Gradually, God pulled him out of the deep hole of despair he was in. And, out of this experience came one of the greatest hymns ever written. Martin poured his soul over the words which became known as the Battle Hymn of the Reformation. You know this hymn as "A Mighty Fortress Is Our God." His faith was renewed. He picked up his work again and pressed on.

Sadly, less than two years later, my second child, Elizabeth, born during an outbreak of the plague, died at only eight months of age. It was so difficult to lose my precious little angel. But, together we persevered. Our faith, once again, sustained us.

Let me tell you a little about dear Martin. Of course, he was the leader of the Protestant Reformation. And as I said, he was a professor and a parish priest. But, he was so much more than that. He loved to talk, to discuss, to argue. One of his greatest joys was the very lively discussions he held around the dinner table. The subject of these talks was virtually anything, everything under the sun. Very well-known guests frequently attended these *table talks*. And Martin always included me in these talks, treating me as an equal, though my knowledge of Latin and the scriptures were certainly not equal to his. Yet, he encouraged me to participate, treating me as an equal, even though I was a woman.

But, his greatest joy was music. He had earned money to pay for his schooling expenses by playing the lute and singing on the streets of Eisebech. In later years, he became a well-recognized musician, though he did not like the organ, trumpets or drum, all of which he called "a terrible shouting to the honor of God." His instrument of choice was the lute, which he believed the angels were playing as they were singing in the revelation Saint John described in his vision. Sir Doctor said, more than once, that "the one who sings prays double." He was such a passionate singer, he was sometimes called the "Nightingale of Wittenberg."

In a way, he invented the Protestant hymn, writing over 37 hymns. Oh, there had been German hymns, but they were only sung outdoors, on pilgrimage, or at a grave site, not within the sanctuary of the church, which was forbidden by order of the Council of Basel. Dr. Luther felt so strongly about the power of singing that he held singing lessons for children and adults alike. He once said that "children must sing and learn music together with mathematics." You see, he believed that songs have a stronger influence than the spoken text because the lyrics, joined with the melody, enters straight into the soul.

On one occasion, Martin wrote these words: "Next to the word of God, music deserves the highest praise. She is a mistress and governess of those human emotions… which control men, or more often, overwhelm them… whether you wish to comfort the sad, to subdue frivolity, to encourage the despairing, to humble the proud, to calm the passionate, or to appease those full of hate… what more effective means than music could you find?"[2]

He took the words of those hymns very seriously. For a basically illiterate people, it was a way to teach the people the Bible stories, as well as the basic tenets of the Christian faith. He wrote hymns for every church season, for the teaching of the catechism and for memorization of scripture as he put many of the psalms to music, much like that song writer, Mr. Charles Wesley, would do two centuries later.

2 Luther's Works, vol. 53: *Liturgy and Hymns*, ed. Juroslav Jan Petikan, Hilton C. Oswald, and Helmutt T. Lehmann (Philadelphia; Fortress Press, 1999)

These are some of the things he was passionate about. Though our marriage was harmonious, we were certainly opposites in many ways. As I have said, he was passionate about books: reading them, writing them, teaching them. He was passionate about music. He was passionate about his theological discussions over dinner.

What he was not passionate about was supervising the livestock enterprise, making cheese or beer, working in the gardens and fields, getting dirt under his fingernails. He was happy to turn those responsibilities over to me.

A part of my duties included serving meals for thirty or forty people regularly, providing banquets for more than a hundred guests, and on occasion, nursing the sick, for I was a skilled nurse. I often made my own medicines from my garden, and people came from all around to purchase my homemade remedies. Occasionally, as various epidemics spread through the land, I opened up Black Cloister as a temporary hospital. All of this I did while rearing six children and being the pastor's wife to the best known pastor in Germany, if not in the whole world. Without meaning to, I became the role model for a pastor's wife. To accomplish all this, it was necessary to rise at 4:00 each morning, not to fulfill the "perfect wife" mentioned in the book of Proverbs, but because I needed the extra hours to get everything done. My husband dubbed me the "Morning Star of Wittenberg."

The Reformation gave new dignity to the Christian woman by recognizing domestic work as a form of ministry. Martin and I saw all of life as spiritual, not distinguishing between "practical" and "spiritual." Therefore, one's calling was not superior over the other.

As I said in the beginning, it was the best of times, it was the worst of times. As wars raged, we were forced to leave Black Cloister three different times. Once, when we returned, we found that our home and property was almost completely destroyed and most of the animals either stolen or killed. The following year, our crops failed.

Then, we lost our daughter Magdalena at thirteen years of age. I didn't think anything could hurt worse than the death of our precious eight month old. But Lena's death rocked both of us to the core, especially Martin. Dear Lena died in his arms after a lingering illness. Martin was almost overcome with both grief and guilt. Over and over he would say, "I know I should be rejoicing that Lena is free from pain and safe in the arms of Jesus. But rejoice, I cannot. The spirit is willing, but the flesh is weak." But, we had our faith. We had our God. And, our God is a mighty fortress, a bulwark never failing, our helper amid a flood of mortal ills.

My beloved Martin died in 1546, just four years after our daughter's death. In time, he had made peace with God, but his health was broken. He was buried underneath the pulpit of Castle Church at Wittenberg. (I understand it is a popular tourist attraction in that city to this day.)

I had thought I would inherit all his holdings at his death, since his will clearly stated such. But, because of some technically with Saxon law, that did not happen. Times were tough, but my faith never wavered. I was often heard saying, "I will stick to Christ as a burr to cloth."

It gave me joy to see my youngest daughter, Margareta, marry into a noble and wealthy family. And, would you believe, one of her descendents became president of Germany in 1932.

Yes, my life was full of ups and downs, good times and not-so-good times. But through it all I've learned to trust in Jesus, I've learned to trust in God, I've learned to depend upon God's word. Dear friends, a mighty fortress is our God. He is our helper amid whatever comes against us. What he did for me, he'll do for you, if you will only allow him to move in your life.

Again, thank you for inviting me here today.

SAINT TERESA OF AVILA

Character: *Saint Teresa of Avila (1515-1582)*

Caption: *The Barefoot Nun of Spain*

Publicity Blurb: *Who would believe that a petite, sickly woman, given to flights of ecstasy which some considered madness, could lead a reform within the great Catholic Church?*

Scripture: *2 Corinthians 12:1-10*

"Prayer for True Life" reprinted in United Methodist Hymnal (p. 403)

Hymns: *"Jesu, Joy Of Man's Desiring"; "More Love To Thee"; "O Master, Let Me Walk With Thee"; "Make Me A Captive, Lord"; "Be Thou My Vision"*

Length of Performance: *word count 2,907 Approximately 20 minutes*

Dress: *16ᵗʰ century Carmelite Habit — can use plain black cleric or choir Robe; "Wimple", a white one piece, heavily starched, cloth worn over head, hair and neck, pulled tightly completely framing the face; White "neckerchief" worn over robe, covering shoulders and hanging down almost to waist; Black "veil" (not worn over face) but cape-like, covering head and draping to just below shoulders.*

Accessories: *large silver cross necklace; plain Silver ring; black robe belt with rosary attached. rosary **never** worn as necklace.*

(Portrait available online)

Shoes: *barefoot — No Shoes! Discalceate Carmelite nuns were known for wearing no shoes.*

Suggested Season to Perform: *St. Teresa Feast Day, October 15*

Saint Teresa Of Avila

The "Barefoot Nun" of Spain

Hello, my name is Teresa Sanchez de Cepeda y Ahumada, but I go simply by the name of Teresa. I was born in 1515 in Avila, Spain. My grandfather was a Jewish convert to Christianity, which caused him to be condemned by the Spanish Inquisition because they accused him of returning to the Jewish faith. But he never did.

His son-in-law, my father, was one of the wealthiest men in Avila. He was so rich he was able to buy his knighthood and so, was readily accepted into the Christian community. My mother made sure that my brother and sister and I were raised as pious Christians.

My mother loved to read fiction, especially romance novels. My father greatly objected to these frivolous books, which he called trash. Mother had taught me to never lie, but she encouraged me not to tell my father about the books. That really put me in the middle, but I didn't want to cause more problems for my mother, so I kept her secret.

Growing up, I was fascinated by the accounts of the saints of the church. When I was seven years old, I convinced my brother to run away with me to find the Moors and be beheaded. That way I could become a saint myself. Fortunately, though unfortunately I thought, we were caught by our uncle and returned home.

Mother died when I was eleven. In my grief, I turned to a deep devotion to the Virgin Mary, seeing her now as my spiritual mother. Along with this deep religious devotion, I was also enamored with popular fiction, especially tales of brave knights. But, when I reached my teenage years, all I cared about was boys, clothes, flirting, and rebellion. I'm sure things have changed by now.

At sixteen, my father thought I was out of control, and chose to send me to the Carmelite convent there at Avila for my education. At first, I hated the convent, but found that it was actually less strict than the rule of my father.

When it came time for me to be married, I faced a dilemma. My choice was to marry or to become a nun. That was a hard choice for me. I had watched my mother suffer through a very difficult marriage. But, nuns didn't seem to have much fun either. Finally, I felt the cloistered life of a nun was the only safe place for someone as prone to sin I was.

As a nun, I prayed as hard as I could to keep Jesus within me at all times. For eighteen years, I prayed this way without much success. I had thought the convent would be a safe place for me to develop the spiritual life. It was not. Many women, who had no place else to go, wound up at the convent, whether they had received a calling or not. They would arrange their veils attractively and wear jewelry. There was a steady stream of visitors in the parlor of the convent with parties that included young men. In spite of myself, I got involved in flattery, vanity, and gossip.

Then, the illnesses began. I came down with malaria. After a seizure, I went into a deep coma for four days. When I awoke, I found out they had already dug my grave. Afterward, I was paralyzed for three years and I never was ever completely well again. You would think that my sickness would draw me deeper into my spiritual life. Instead, it became an excuse for me to stop praying all together. The illness distracted me from yielding myself completely to God.

Finally, I was able to pray again. But I did not pray boldly. Early in my illness, I turned to God for strength and relief from pain. During times of intense prayer, I often experienced a type of religious ecstasy. I found this mystical state both exhilarating and frightening. But after a while, the feeling of ecstasy faded and I entered a state of humility where I felt I was not worthy to come before God in prayer — that I was too great a sinner. I felt like the apostle Paul when he claimed that he was the chief of sinners. For years, I hardly prayed at all, feeling that as a wicked sinner, I didn't deserve to get favors from God. During this time, I began to inflict various tortures and mortifications of the flesh, or flagellations, upon myself. I, now, believe that obedience to God is more important than penance. If you do something wrong, don't punish yourself — change!

When I was 41, I was persuaded by a compassionate priest to return to my previous deep devotion to the Virgin Mary. It was during this time that I became convinced that Jesus Christ presented himself to me in bodily form, though invisible. These visions lasted almost uninterrupted for more than two years. In one of these visions, a seraph drove the fiery point of a golden spear repeatedly through my heart, causing great spiritual and bodily pain. This spear seemed to reach into my innermost entrails. And when he withdrew it, he seemed to draw my entrails also, leaving me all on fire with a great love of God. The pain was so great that it made me moan. And yet, as incredibly unbearable as this pain was, there was a sweetness about it that I did not want to lose.

This vision was so strong that it served as an inspiration throughout the rest of my life and motivated me with my lifelong imitation of the life and suffering of Jesus, so much so that my motto actually became, *"Lord, either let me suffer or let me die."*

There were those in the church who concluded that I had been deceived by the devil, that the devil was the one coming to me in my visions. They sent a Jesuit to analyze me, and then a counselor to hear my confession. On one occasion, my confessor was so sure that the visions were from the devil that he told me to make the obscene gesture called the "fig" every time I had a vision of my Jesus. You may not be familiar with the term "fig", but it is an ancient gesture where the thumb is thrust between the two adjoining fingers, similar to your present-day gesture of a similar nature.

Oh, I didn't want to do it, to do something so profane in the presence of such holiness and purity. But I had taken a vow of obedience to my spiritual leaders, and so did as I was ordered, all the time apologizing to Jesus. But you know what? When I talked this over with Jesus, he wasn't upset. You see, Jesus knew my heart and Jesus knew of the great love that I felt for him. He even told me that I was right to obey my superior. Sometimes, I think I'm more afraid of those who are terrified of the devil that I am of the devil himself. The devil is not all-powerful. The devil can be subdued, can be sent away, through prayer.

Eventually, that counselor gave up and let me proceed as usual with my spiritual life. He had attempted to prove that my visions were not from God. But, I never needed any proof that they were from God. Only God could give me the peace and joy which came from the visions. Only God can give that *peace which passes all understanding.*

After residing for a while in the Augustinian convent, in 1535 I entered the Carmelite Monastery of the Incarnation in Avila. I was greatly troubled by what I saw. There were so many visitors, many of high social and political rank, that the experience of solitude was almost nonexistent. I resolved to correct the abuses I saw. Perhaps, I had been influenced by the former monk, Martin Luther, and his movement of the Protestant Reformation, some twenty years earlier. I set about doing what I could where I could. For many years, I worked encouraging Spanish Jewish converts to follow Christianity.

I realized there was only so much I could do within the monastery where I lived. Therefore, I took on the mission to form new convents. My plan was the revival of the earlier, stricter rules such as weekly flagellations, as much pious seclusion as possible, and the discalceation of the nuns. That word "discalceation" simply means "un-shoed." The Carmelite order had taken up this custom based on a religious group which was formed at Mount Carmel in Israel which followed this practice. It was a visible sign of humility. However, when plans leaked out about establishing the first convent, I was denounced from the pulpit and threatened with punishment from the Inquisition. The townspeople actually started legal proceedings against me. Yet, all this publicity only seemed to give more attention to my cause.

During this time of establishing these new orders, or convents, I made frequent journeys throughout nearly all the provinces of Spain. My journeys were twofold: first, to establish these new convents, and second to raise money for the poor in our country. I had a real passion to be able to purchase shoes for the poor children who had none, even during the harsh winter months. Those who like to make fun of religious persons of devotion dubbed me *The Barefoot Nun of Spain.* Though I was shoeless, you might find it interesting to know that if I wore shoes, it would be only a size four. This only emphasizes that the size of the feet does not matter. It is the size of the devotion which is most important. Of course, I never made any of those trips without my portable statue of the Christ Child to help me focus my thoughts always on Jesus.

When someone asked me what to do when they were depressed, I replied that, of course, one should pray. But in addition to prayer, I would suggest that they go someplace where they could see the sky and take a walk. The fresh air, the benefits of walking, the sights of God's creation all around, dispels the darkness and gloom that can weigh on a person.

On my many journeys, I braved burning sun, ice and snow, thieves, and rat–infested inns in order to find more of these reformed convents. And yet, all those hardships paled when compared to the persecution I faced from my brothers and sisters in the religious life. Many of them called me "a reckless disobedient gadabout who has gone about teaching as though she were a professor." As I have often said, "May God protect me from gloomy saints."

In 1576, a series of persecutions against me, my friends and my reforms were started by the older Carmelite order. By executive order, I was forbidden to found any additional convent, and I was condemned to voluntary retirement. During this time, I was ordered to write a book. Many people questioned my experiences and the church officials felt that this book would clear me or condemn me. I did as I was told, but because of this, I used a lot of camouflage in the book. Following a profound thought, I would remark with the statement, "But what do I know? I'm just a wretched woman." Believe it or not, it worked.

Finally, after three years I was brought before the Spanish Inquisition, which had read my work, and they liked what I had written! My charges were dropped, as were my prior restrictions, and I was allowed to continue with my reforms. In total, seventeen convents and almost as many men's cloisters were formed.

This exercise in writing led me to author my autobiography. In it, I listed the Ascent of the Soul in four stages:

The first is the *Devotion of the Heart*. This is mental prayer of profound concentration and contemplation. It centers especially on the devout observance of the passion of Christ. It is my belief that mental prayer is nothing less than an intimate sharing between friends. It means taking time, frequently, to be alone with Christ, who we know loves us. The important thing is not to *think* much, but to *love* much.

The second is the *Devotion of Peace*. This is where the human will is surrendered to God. In this supernatural state, faculties such as memory and reason are not yet removed from worldly distractions. While outside occurrences cannot be completely avoided, there is the prevailing state of quietude.

The third is the *Devotion of Union*. It is absorption in God. Here, one is able to absorb much more of the reason of God and enter into a conscious, all-encompassing rapture in the love of God.

The fourth is the *Devotion of the Ecstasy*. This is where consciousness of being in the body disappears. One is so absorbed into God that one does not know where they end and God begins. Body and spirit are in the throes of a sweet, happy pain, alternating between unconsciousness and an ecstatic flight, in which the body is literally lifted into space. After about a half an hour, profound relaxation occurs, which lasts for a few hours where one is in a swoon-like weakness similar to a trance. It has been said by some that they have occasionally observed me levitating during the mass.

Over the years I wrote three major books: my autobiography, *The Life of Teresa of Jesus, The Interior Castle,* and *The Way of Perfection,* plus countless shorter writings on prayer, the devotional life, Christian meditation and Christian mysticism. In my later writings on mysticism, I attempted to analyze and dissect mystical experiences the way a scientist would. I give thanks to God for my ability to write these books. It is only one of the many gifts my God has seen fit to bestow on me. Of course, I received no money for these publications, for I had taken a vow of poverty. All the money went to the church.

Never would I have believed that, centuries later, in your day actually, I would be declared a doctor of the church for my writing and teaching on prayer. Only one other woman has ever been honored in this way.

Regardless of all my writings on the importance of prayer and the power of prayer, I firmly believe that the most powerful and acceptable prayer is that prayer which leads to action. The apostle Paul wrote that, "Faith without good works is dead." I might paraphrase his words to say: "Prayer without works is ineffectual." As much as I am enamored with the state of ecstasy that I often achieve in prayer, I must reiterate that prayer that leads to action is even more to be preferred.

Are you familiar with the poem by Annie Flint, "Christ has no hands but our hands to do his work today. He has no feet but our feet to lead men in the way"? These are beautiful words and I certainly cannot write poetry like that. But perhaps my words influenced her poem. At one point, I had written, "Christ has no body but yours, no hands, no feet on earth but yours. Yours are the eyes with which He looks with compassion on this world. Yours are the feet with which He walks to do good. Yours are the hands with which he blesses all the world. Yours are the hands, yours are the feet, yours are the eyes, you are his body. Christ had no body now on earth but yours."

Thank you again, for inviting me here to speak with you. I have a prayer which I pray almost every day. Often, when I go to speak to a group, I close with this prayer. And so, I'd like to close with this prayer. Let us pray....

Oh Lord, govern all by thy wisdom, so that my soul may always be serving thee as thou dost will it, and not as I may choose. Do not punish me, I beseech thee, by granting that which I wish or ask if it offend thy love. Let me die to myself, that I may serve thee. Let me live to thee, who in thyself art the true life. Amen.

Thank you.

SOJOURNER TRUTH

Character: *Sojourner Truth (1797-1883)*

Caption: *Friend of Freedom*

Publicity Blurb: *"Can you imagine a child born into slavery rising to such prominence that you were invited to meet with **two** United States presidents to discuss your work?"*

Scripture Read: *Isaiah 6:1-8*

Hymns: *"Here I Am, Lord"; "Lord, Speak To Me"; "The Voice Of God Is Calling";"O Young And Fearless Prophet"*

Length of Performance: *word count 3,848 Approximately 25 minutes*

Dress: *floor length, long sleeve, plain neck, dark homespun cotton dress, loosely gathered at a low waist.*

Hair: *white, civil war style sun bonnet*

Shoes: *lace-up short boots*

Accessories: *white "neckerchief", a rectangle of crisp linen, 30" x 40", wrapped around neck and ends crossed over in front and secured with a safety pin, with added fringed, black short crocheted shawl.*

(Portrait available online)

Props: *wooden walking stick*

Suggested Season to Perform: *Black History month*

Sojourner Truth

Hello, thank you for inviting me here to share my story with you. My name is Isabella Baumfree, but you know me better by my adoptive name, Sojourner Truth. I was born into slavery in 1797 in upstate New York. My parents had both been brought over from Ghana.

In my early years, I spoke only Dutch. That led to many beatings because I did not understand quickly enough how to follow the commands given me. At the age of ten, after tying my hands, I was beaten so severely by my owner, John Nealy, that I bear the scars to this day. Not long after, I was purchased by an equally cruel master Mr. Dumont. The abuse I endured from him was severe, and not only from him but from his wife in ways I won't go into.

Alone on the Dumont farm, with little contact with other blacks, I found my own way to worship God. I built a temple of brush in the woods, an African tradition I learned from my mother. There, I engaged in almost mystical experiences, again influenced by my mother, where I bargained with God as if he were a familiar presence.

Over the years, I was sold five times. In 1827, New York State abolished slavery for adults over forty years of age. Four years earlier, I took my infant daughter, Sophia, and we left my master, leaving my other four children behind because the New York Emancipation Order did not permit anyone's freedom until they had served as a bound servant for twenty years. Dumont said I ran away, but the truth is I walked away and in the light of day.

Isaac and Maria Van Wagenen took me in and purchased me for the sum of $20.00. They were a deeply religious couple and taught me much of the Christian faith. Under their leadership and influence, I experienced a profound religious conversion.

While living with the Van Wagenens, I received word that Dumont had illegally sold my five-year-old son, Peter, into slavery in Alabama. I sued in court, and with the help of the Wagenens, was able to gain my son back. I became the first black woman to win such a case against a white man.

But, though I won my case and got my son back, I was consumed with revenge. I called upon God to punish that family who had bought my child and had laughed when I had tried to get him back. But when that man, Fowler Gedney, murdered his wife and his mother-in-law went insane, I became convinced in my power with God and terrified at the terrible vengeance I had brought upon my persecutors. I cried out, "That's too much, God! I did not mean quite so much!" I have been more careful with my prayers since then.

The Van Wagenens helped me let go of that hatred. They were a good Methodist family and, in addition to teaching me the faith, told me much of what had happened years earlier in England in the fight against slavery. They told an amazing story about a Mr. William Wilberforce who worked for over twenty years in Parliament to abolish slavery. On the night before the crucial vote was taken, a friend visited him and found Mr. Wilberforce in some turmoil. He asked if Wilberforce had changed his mind against the practice of slavery. He said no. He was asked if Wilberforce was concerned that his stand might end his political career. He said no. "Then what is the problem?" he asked. Wilberforce replied, "I just hate to be called one of those Methodists." I appreciate the Methodist and Quaker involvement in the anti-slavery movement, both in England and in this country.

For a while, I attended the white Methodist meetings with the Van Wagenens, and then found an African Methodist Church, known as the AME Church, to affiliate with. Over the years, I participated with many different religious groups, some with good results, some not so good. I moved to New York City and found work as a domestic with a wealthy merchant by the name of Elijah Pierson and his wife. A very charismatic man named Robert Matthews convinced the Piersons to join his group. I went with them, though I was the only black in that community. I found out that it was a cult, with all the trademarks of a cult. This Mr. Matthews renamed himself Mathias and claimed to be a direct descendant of Matthew of the New Testament. He ordered his followers to turn over all their worldly assets to him and he decided who would sleep with whom. He, of course, took his pick.

There were frequent beatings for disobedience to his will. The beatings were hard, but not new to me. But, when Mr. Pierson was poisoned because his wealth was not enough to satisfy Mathias, Mathias was arrested, though never indicted. He soon disappeared, but not before accusing me of attempting to poison others. I was never indicted and I later filed suit for slander and collected $125.00. My second victory in the courts!

After that, I spent some time in the utopian community in Sing Sing, New York, time with the Millerites, an offshoot of Pentecostal Methodism which eventually led to the Seventh Day Adventists, and with others. But, most of the groups were very affirming, especially the Quakers and the Methodists. And, I found that, while some were better than others, no *one* group seems to have *all* the truth. I came to believe that there is room for many different expressions in the way we worship our God. I find that I like a quote from the Methodist founder, John Wesley, who said "For opinions' sake, let us not argue. If your heart is right, give me your hand. Come, let us worship together." After all, our country was built on freedom of religion.

Like thousands of slaves and free blacks, and poor whites, I was swept up by the tide of the Second Great Awakening. I felt "baptized in the Holy Spirit" and received a vision from God where I recognized Jesus as my soul-protecting fortress and was given the power to rise above the battlements of fear. Having gained my freedom, I worked for many years as a domestic with several different families.

While living in New York, I attended many camp meetings. And in 1843, on the day of Pentecost, God's Holy Spirit spoke to me right on the streets of Brooklyn. His spirit instructed me to leave New York, a "Second Sodom", and travel to lecture under the name of "Sojourner". I heard him whisper that name! And so, I took that name. I added the name "Truth" because I understood that my mission was to teach people to embrace Jesus and refrain from sin, and to speak out in truth against injustice wherever I found it. As I told my friends, "The Spirit calls me, and I must go." My speeches, in the beginning, were not political. My speaking was based on my unique interpretation of the Bible — based on my experiences as a woman and an ex-slave.

I began my ministry by strolling into churches and other public meetings asking to be heard. And, in spite of my rough appearance, and with the power of the Holy Spirit, more often than not, I was allowed to speak. I never knew where my next meal would come from or where I would sleep. Sometimes, I was invited to stay at the homes of wealthy listeners. But as likely as not, I would spend the next night in a barn.

During my speaking engagements, I wore, across my chest, a satin banner with the words: "Proclaim Liberty Throughout The Land Unto The Inhabitants Thereof." I received some fame and some infamy. I usually spoke to mainly white audiences, some who were favorable to my views and some who were not.

At one speaking engagement with the United Brethren, I found out the hard way that this meeting had been infiltrated by a mob led by a local physician. As I was passionately proclaiming the truth, I was interrupted by this heckler who shouted out, "You ain't no woman." He demanded that I bare my breasts to a committee of women to prove my sex. Before I could even respond, he demanded a vote on whether I was a man or a woman. By an overwhelming majority, the jeering crowd voted that I was a man!

I had heard this accusation before, possibly because I certainly did not act like a demure female, possibly because I had a strong bass voice, and possibly because I stood almost six feet tall. I know I'm not that tall now, but as many of you have found out, often a person shrinks as one ages. On this day, this accusation hit me wrong. Here I was proclaiming the truth about all these injustices and I became angry. Do you remember the time Moses got angry and struck the rock? Well, I did not strike a rock, but I did strike out in anger. I shouted out, "I show my breasts to the whole congregation! It ain't my shame, but yours that I should do this. Here, then, see for yourselves!" and I opened my shirt and exposed my breasts. It silenced the hecklers, but it also broke up the meeting. I never did that again. I asked God for forgiveness for my outburst.

On my lecture circuit, I tried not to be boring. A man once told me, "It is a sin to be boring when you are sharing God's

Word." Good advice, I think. And so, in addition to proclaiming the truth and speaking to support my various passions, I also told stories, sang songs and psalms, and interjected as much humor as seemed appropriate, so that one would leave not only inspired and educated, but also entertained.

As I said, in the beginning my speeches were not political. But, I found out quickly that God's truth *is* political. My passion ranged from speaking out for the abolition of slavery, for women's rights and suffrage, for the rights of freedmen, for temperance, for religious freedom, for prison reform, and for the termination of capital punishment.

In 1850, I was able to publish my autobiography, *The Narrative of Sojourner Truth: A Northern Slave*. Of course, since I could neither read nor write, I found it necessary to dictate my book. The proceeds from the book, and subsequent speaking engagements, enabled me to purchase a modest home. Though I never was active in the Underground Railroad, I supported the movement and helped as many newly freed slaves as I could by finding housing for them. I was interviewed by Harriet Beecher Stowe for an article she wrote about me in the *Atlantic Monthly* magazine which allowed me to reach many people with my views.

When the newfangled invention of photography became accessible to common folk, I was encouraged to sell photographs of myself to supplement the income from my book and lectures. Though the word photograph takes its name from the word for light, in fact the pictures were kind of dark, full of black and white and shadows, so much so that some people referred to them as shadows. And so I said, "I sell the shadow to support the substance."

One of my passions was women's rights and suffrage, the right of a woman to vote. Why shouldn't a woman have the same rights as a man? Isn't a woman equal to a man? Doesn't the Bible say, "So God created man in his own image, in the image of God created he him; male and female created he them" (Genesis 1:27). Doesn't that sound like God thought they were equal?

At a women's suffrage convention in 1851, a number of ministers had invaded the meeting hall uninvited and monopolized the discussion, quoting biblical texts to the effect that women should shun all activities except those of childbearing, homemaking and subservience to their husbands. I sat still for several hours on the pulpit steps listening patiently to this masculine filibuster. When I could take it no long, I jumped up and gave what was to become my most famous speech titled, "And Ain't I a Woman?" At the end of my speech, the disruptive clergymen were silenced.

There seems to be several variations of that speech. I cannot verify exactly which one is the most correct. That speech was extemporaneous. Ain't that a fancy word? It just means that I spoke in the passion of the moment, not from some memorized text. My words probably came from the abolitionists' rallying cry, "I am a man." This phrase refers to the practice of white folk calling our full-grown black men as *boys*, implying that they are inferior to white *men*, just like they call me *girl* and I ain't been a girl in a lot of years. I understand that this slogan was picked up and used in your day by sanitation workers in your city of Memphis.

As well as I remember, the speech went something like this:

"Well, children, where there is so much racket there must be something out of kilter. I think that 'twixt the Negroes of the south and the women in the north, all talking about rights, the white men will be in a fix pretty soon. But what's all this here talking about? That man over there says that women need to be helped into carriages, and lifted over ditches, and to have the best place everywhere! Nobody ever gets me into carriages, or over mud puddles, or gives me any best place and ain't I a woman?

"Look at me. Look at my arms. I have plowed and planted, and gathered into barns, as any man. And ain't I a woman?

"I can work as much as a man and eat as much as a man — when I can get it — and bear the lash as well. And ain't I a woman?"

"I have borne five children, and seen most all sold off into slavery, and when I cried out with my mother's grief, none but Jesus heard me! And ain't I a woman?

"Then they talk about this thing in the head. What they call it? Intellect, that's it, intellect. What's that got to do with women's

179

rights or Negro rights. Then that little man said to me, 'Women can't have as much right as men 'cause Christ wasn't a woman.' Let me ask you, 'Where did your Christ come from? Where did your Christ come from? From God and a *woman!* Man had nothing to do with him.'

"If the first woman God ever made was strong enough to turn the world upside down all alone, these women together ought to be able to turn it back, and set it right side up again. And now they is asking to do it and the men better let them."

At a 1852 conference in Boston where several abolitionists were speaking, I was greatly offended at the pessimistic tone of the esteemed Mr. Frederick Douglass. He stated that the white people of America would never put an end to the Negro's bondage. There was only one answer, and that was an armed revolt by the slaves themselves, which could only result in wholesale slaughter. He was frustrated that God had not liberated the slaves. I took it as long as I could and I jumped to my feet, interrupting his speech, and asked him, "Why, Mr. Douglass, is God gone?" What I meant by that was that God *was* active in this movement. An avalanche of applause swept away the despair that had hung over the room. Various writers elaborated on this exchange and made me almost a symbol for faith in non-violence and God's power to right the wrongs of slavery. (Maybe my words influenced Dr. Martin Luther King Jr. so many years later.)

During the Civil War, I was granted an appointment with President Lincoln to plead with him to allow free men of color to help fight in the war. While I was there at the White House, Mr. Lincoln showed me the Lincoln Bible, which had been given to him by the black people of Baltimore. I was able to return to the White House several times to renew my plea. Finally, the President and Congress agreed. And, I helped to recruit black troops and lead campaigns to raise food and clothing for black regiments. I stayed on in Washington for a while nursing wounded soldiers and finding food and shelter for the homeless, emancipated slaves who were pouring into the capital.

After the war, I became involved with the Freedman's Bureau, helping freed slaves find jobs and build new lives. While in

Washington, I lobbied against segregation, and when a streetcar conductor violently blocked me from riding on the streetcar, I ensured his arrest and won my case. My third court victory! (Maybe, I became an inspiration for Rosa Parks so many years later.)

After Mr. Grant became president, I was privileged to meet with him as I checked on the progress of the rights of former slaves seeking to secure land grants from the federal government. My dream was for these former slaves to be given free land out west, with the possibility of creating a Negro state. Though I collected over a thousand signatures on a petition to provide former slaves with land and went through the monumental stack of paperwork to ensure a bill to that end, Congress never took action. I found out later that the bill was never even submitted to Congress. My popularity began to fade after these efforts — among the whites who didn't want all this free land given to blacks, and among blacks who objected to a segregated state instead of full integration.

In 1879, the Exodusters Movement (named from Moses and his exodus from slavery) caused a rush of freed blacks from the south to migrate to the west, primarily Colorado, Oklahoma, and Kansas, escaping the violent Reconstruction era and the Ku Klux Klan. Kansas was the choice spot because they had fought so hard to become a free state.

I eventually settled in Battle Creek, Michigan, near my family. One day a child, seeing how very old I was, asked me, "Ms. Sojourner, are you afraid of dying?" I looked at this dear child and said, "I ain't goin' to die, honey. When my time comes, I'm goin' home like a shootin' star!"

I had many struggles. Through the years, there were frequent attempts to silence me and my message. I was stoned and beaten on more than one occasion. But, through it all, my Jesus did prove to be my soul-protecting fortress and I was given the power to rise above the battlements of fear, just as the Spirit had promised.

I saw my struggles similar to Moses' struggles. Remember how Moses led his people all the way to the Red Sea? But, then, here come the soldiers — the soldiers behind and the sea in front.

What to do? Pray! And pray he did — all night long. And the sea parted, and dry land appeared with water piled up on the sides. A frightening sight. And Moses and the people just stood there. Then, God said to Moses, "Quit praying and get moving!" And they did. But it was still scary.

And what they crossed over into was not the promised land. It was a wilderness with no milk and honey. It was wandering with no home, no crops, dependent on God, literally, for their daily bread.

I saw the plight of the freed slaves similar. I saw that we still had a lot of work to do. They needed a place to live, jobs, food, freedom from prejudice. A lot of work still to do.

Yes, I 'spect there is still work to be done for the abolition to the slavery of strong drink which destroys family, friends and finances.

Yes, I 'spect there is still work to be done for the abolition of religious intolerance which pits one Christian group against another Christian group, thinking that their way is the only way.

Yes, I 'spect there is still work to be done for the abolition of religious intolerance against one God-fearing group of folk against another God-fearing folk 'cause they call God by another name.

Yes, I 'spect there is still work to be done for the abolition of cruelty to prisoners who are treated like animals in a cage, instead of men and women created in the image of God.

Yes, I 'spect there is still work to be done for the abolition of capital punishment, remembering that only God can *give* life, and so, only God should be the one to *take* life.

Yes, I 'spect there is still work to be done.

I heard God calling me to sojourn throughout the land and proclaim truth wherever I found it. And, with God's help, that is what I have tried to do.

But, God didn't call only me. God called each of you to proclaim truth and speak out against injustice wherever you find it. And, with God's help you, too, can do just that.

Well, that's all I got to say. Thank you, again, for inviting me to speak with you.

www.ingramcontent.com/pod-product-compliance
Lightning Source LLC
Chambersburg PA
CBHW021402090426
42742CB00009B/970